The Sonnets of Rainer Maria Rilke

Other Books of Interest from St. Augustine's Press

John Poch, *God's Poems: The Beauty of Poetry and the Christian Imagination*

Gene Fendt, *Camus' Plague: Myth for Our World*

David K. O'Connor, *Plato's Bedroom: Ancient Wisdom and Modern Love*

Marvin R. O'Connell, *Telling Stories that Matter: Memoirs and Essays*

Joseph Bottum, *The Second Spring*

Joseph Bottum, *The Fall and Other Poems*

Peter Kreeft, *Socrates' Children: The 100 Greatest Philosophers*

Peter Kreeft, *Ethics for Beginners: Big Ideas from 32 Great Minds*

Jeremy Black, *The Importance of Being Poirot*

Nathan Lefler, *Tale of a Criminal Mind Gone Good*

Nalin Ranasinghe, *The Confessions of Odysseus*

Will Morrisey, *Herman Melville's Ship of State*

Roger Scruton, *The Politics of Culture and Other Essays*

Roger Scruton, *The Meaning of Conservatism: Revised 3rd Edition*

Roger Scruton, *An Intelligent Person's Guide to Modern Culture*

David Lowenthal, *Slave State: Rereading Orwell's 1984*

Stanley Rosen, *The Language of Love: An Interpretation of Plato's Phaedrus*

Winston Churchill, *The River War*

The Sonnets of Rainer Maria Rilke

Translated and Introduced by
Rick Anthony Furtak

St. Augustine's Press
South Bend, Indiana

Manufactured in the United States of America.

1 2 3 4 5 6 27 26 25 24 23 22

Library of Congress Control Number: 2021949572

Paperback ISBN: 978-1-58731-845-0
Ebook ISBN 978-1-58731-846-7

∞ The paper used in this publication meets the minimum requirements of the American National Standard for Information Sciences – Permanence of Paper for Printed Materials, ANSI Z39.48-1984.

St. Augustine's Press
www.staugustine.net

to R.R.T. and J.D.R.
German and Germanic loved ones
who inspire me

CONTENTS

Translator's Introduction:
Rilke, Poetic Form, and the Revelation of Meaning

Rick Anthony Furtak

Rainer Maria Rilke's sonnets are an accomplishment of both *vision* and *voice*, a way of seeing and a way of speaking. I will begin with a brief word about each of these notions before dealing with them in greater depth. In a paper written twenty years after Rilke's death – "Wozu Dichter?," or "What Are Poets For?" – Martin Heidegger laments our situation as one in which the meaning of things is hidden or obscured.[1] Consequently, we are in need of poets who can restore a world that once again feels significant. Rilke himself notes in various letters that the poet's task is to reveal the valences of existence, enabling his readers to become and remain emotionally aware of meaning in life despite all that may threaten our sense that our existence is indeed significant. Insofar as the *Sonnets to Orpheus*, and numerous other sonnets (from the *New Poems*, in particular) give voice to this anti-nihilistic or newly enchanted way of seeing the world, they embody Rilke's attempt to realize a mode of poetic vision. Every poem constitutes an incarnation of a specific way to view things, one that stresses their emotional connotations – that is, their

1 Heidegger, "What Are Poets For?," trans. by Alfred Hofstadter, in *Poetry, Language, Thought* (New York: Harper Perennial, 2001), 89–139.

affective significance.[2] To adopt such a mode of viewing requires being conscious of axiologically rich features of the world: poetic vision, then, brings tangible value to light for both poet and reader.

As for poetic voice, by this term I intend to designate the musical aspects of any poem written in the sonnet form – in particular, Rilke's distinct way of singing, achieved through his use of the the patterns of meter and sound (especially rhythm, assonance, and rhyme) that are enabled by that structure. These intricate features of language heighten the affective impact of the poet's words, and they often serve to register powerfully felt episodes of recognition that are characterized as having been impressed upon the poet himself. On Rilke's own account, then, the creative process of composing verse involves a kind of receptivity, and its fruits are experienced as an unforeseen gift: in this, he echoes the major nineteenth-century existential philosophers, Søren Kierkegaard and Friedrich Nietzsche, with whom he also shares a belief in the singularity of each individual perspective.[3] In his sonnets, we see how formal constraint can actually be liberating, since it provokes the poet to discover not

2 See, e.g., Maurice Natanson, *The Erotic Bird: Phenomenology in Literature* (Princeton, NJ: Princeton University Press, 1998), 6–7 & 9–10.

3 On how writing is "not voluntary; on the contrary, it is in line with everything in my personality and is its deepest urge," see Kierkegaard, *Journals and Papers: A Selection*, trans. by Alastair Hannay (London: Penguin, 1996), 244. See also Nietzsche's account of inspiration in *Ecce Homo*, trans. by R. J. Hollingdale (London: Penguin, 1992), 72: "One takes, one does not ask who gives; a thought flashes up like lightning, with necessity, unfalteringly formed – I have never had any choice." Regarding individual uniqueness, see Timothy Clark, *The Poetics of Singularity* (Edinburgh: Edinburgh University Press, 2005), 159–160.

only the first words that come to mind but words that disclose something he did not already know. The musical qualities of these poems bring intense feeling and insight emphatically to voice. For these reasons, I will remain attentive throughout my analysis of particular examples to the manner in which Rilke's poetic techniques contribute to his way of articulating a vision of a meaningful and affectively moving world. I shall also make some remarks about what challenges these formal techniques pose for Rilke's translator, and how these can be managed more or less successfully.

1

It is generally known that Rilke's writings have captured the attention of several major philosophical thinkers (including Gadamer and Ricoeur in the twentieth century), and that they are frequently acknowledged as literary contributions to philosophy – worthy of being included in more than one prominent anthology of texts from existential thought. This is fitting enough because, in a Rilkean work such as *The Notebooks of Malte Laurids Brigge*, human life is presented as a state of anguish, confusion, and despair. As the speaker in this novel meditates fearfully on the prospect of death, he questions the meaning of things and struggles in vain to "rub off the make-up" and "be real," to develop an authentic sense of identity.[4] Dread lurks beneath the ordinary routines of daily life, ready at any moment to erupt – for instance, on the face of a stranger in a crowded street. Everything threatens to become radically disorienting as Malte's consciousness is invaded by the noxious, miserable glee of those around him who are desperately trying to enjoy

4 Rilke, *The Notebooks of Malte Laurids Brigge*, trans. by M. D. Herter Norton (New York: W. W. Norton, 1964), 194.

themselves: "I felt that the air had long been exhausted, and that I was now breathing only exhaled breath, which my lungs refused."[5] It all resembles a scene out of Jean-Paul Sartre's *Nausea*, as Rilke explores an unbearable condition for which no evident remedy is available.[6] This awakens a need to find some convincing way to embrace the world nonetheless, affirming it as it is – in something akin to Nietzsche's *amor fati*, love of what is inevitable.[7] As we shall see, Rilke speaks tirelessly about how crucial it is for us to cultivate the outlook we adopt when "we most passionately, most tremblingly affirm our being-here, [and] all that happens."[8] At issue is nothing less than the meaning of life as we human beings know it, and the question of whether or not this life is worth living.

What Heidegger claims, in the essay mentioned above, is that we live in a "destitute" time, one in which the divine radiance of things is hidden from view. Consequently, we are in critical need of poets who can bring the world back to life so that it is once again weighted with tangible significance. In articulating this idea, Heidegger cites Rilke in support of his diagnosis. He quotes a passage where the poet speculates that his generation may be the last to have been acquainted with a real world animated with significance – prior to the nihilistic reign of technology, in which artificial gadgets and contrivances have come to dominate our existence.[9] It is not that

5 *The Notebooks of Malte Laurids Brigge*, 49.

6 Sartre, *Nausea*, trans. by Lloyd Alexander (New York: New Directions, 1964).

7 On this state, in which one "wants nothing to be other than it is," see *Ecce Homo*, 37.

8 Letter of 6 January 1923 to Margot Sizzo, in *The Poet's Guide to Life: The Wisdom of Rilke*, trans. by Ulrich Baer (New York: Modern Library, 2005), 112.

9 Heidegger, "What Are Poets For?," 110–111.

there is anything intrinsically wrong with artifice or technology: the techniques of the artist, rightly understood, can provide a mode of access to meaningful truth. Nevertheless, technical artistry is not often oriented by such noble aims in a culture dominated by utilitarian science. Insofar as the prevailing bias is to regard quantitative measurement as the best means of access to knowledge, our experienced world of color, sound, and emotion is undermined by the presumption that what truly exists is nothing but dull matter devoid of any qualities that should affect us in one way or another. Yet are we doomed, therefore, to be emotionally flat, unimaginative observers who perceive the world as populated only by value-neutral objects? Not necessarily; and poetry has the potential to remind us not to be blinded by the nihilistic assumptions that are easily available to us without thinking.[10]

The poet, by contrast, employs a different method of "taking measure," abiding by the belief that actual qualitative features of the world are disclosed in our emotional experience.[11] Poetry can redeem life by illuminating an aspect of things that is concealed from the scientist's view. It returns us to a world that is fit to be inhabited by human beings, in which meaning has once again become apparent. And, as our sense of reality expands, our affective awareness is broadened. The poet's goal, then, is not to escape from hard facts into a fantasy of his or her own invention. It is, rather, to recognize that "our imagination makes possible

10 Rilke's poetry in particular "invites the possibility of taking a different, mystical perspective on the world." – Ruth Rebecca Tietjen, "Mystical Feelings and the Process of Transformation," *Philosophia* 45 (2017): 1624–1625.

11 Heidegger, *Poetry Language Thought*, 218–221. On how poetry can enable us to see things "as they are anew, under a new aspect, transfigured, subject to a felt variation," see Simon Critchley, *Things Merely Are* (London: Routledge, 2005), 10–12 & 57–58.

the disclosure of reality."[12] Poetry glorifies as it clarifies: its aim is to transform and amplify whatever is there to be perceived, opening up new worlds of tangible meaning as opposed to inert facts. As Rilke writes, "the possibility of intensifying things so that they reveal their essence depends so much on our participation,"[13] and in one of the *New Poems,* as well as *Sonnets to Orpheus* II.4 about "the creature that does not exist," he even flirts with the idea that the creative imagination can perhaps dream something into reality. Yet, in its context, this sonnet is better understood as issuing a rejoinder to all of us, not excepting the poet himself: looking with as much poetic faith as a mustard seed, and with love, we could perhaps move mountains, or at least be moved by such mountains as do exist. As for the unicorn,

> It never *did* exist. But from their love
> this pure being came to be. They gave it room,
> and in that clear space, desolate enough,
> it raised its head up out of the cocoon

12 Colin Falck, *Myth, Truth, and Literature* (Cambridge: Cambridge University Press, 1989), 137–138. The imagination, as Luke Fischer points out, is the faculty which can disclose the world "as animated rather than mechanical": see *The Poet as Phenomenologist: Rilke and the "New Poems"* (London: Bloomsbury Academic, 2015), 92–94 & 221–225. Regarding poetry's capacity for both clarification and glorification, see also Kierkegaard, *Papers and Journals*, 101.

13 Letter of 9 March 1899 to Elena Woronina, in *The Poet's Guide to Life*, 8. Rilke's earlier unicorn poem, "Das Einhorn," is not a sonnet, so is not translated here: for an English version see *New Poems*, trans. by Joseph Cadora (Port Townsend, WA: Copper Canyon Press, 2014), 79.

of nonexistence. So they fed it, not
with grain, but with the possibility
of being. And the creature grew so strong,

out of its brow a single horn emerged.

[Zwar *war* es nicht. Doch weil sie's liebten, ward
ein reines Tier. Sie ließen immer Raum.
Und in dem Raume, klar und ausgespart,
erhob es leicht sein Haupt und brauchte kaum

zu sein. Sie nährten es mit keinem Korn,
nur immer mit der Möglichkeit, es sei.
Und die gab solche Stärke an das Tier,

daß es aus sich ein Stirnhorn trieb. Ein Horn.]

As this poem suggests, some possible beings must be loved in order to be seen as real. Further, a thing that does exist owes its perceptible reality not just to the grain that sustains its body, but to the space of possibilities that it inhabits. Another existential phenomenologist remarks that "the world is what we see,"[14] adding that this item of "faith" should be at home in our ordinary attitudes as well as our philosophical explanations. The Rilkean poet invites us to adopt a point of view from which reality is magical;[15] this is pertinent to perceiving an actual horse (such as the one celebrated in I.20 of *Sonette an Orpheus*), along with

14 Maurice Merleau-Ponty, *The Visible and the Invisible*, trans. by Alphonso Lingis (Evanston, IL: Northwestern University Press, 1968), 3.

15 See, e.g., Theodore Ziolkowski, *Die Welt im Gedicht* (Würzburg: Verlag Köningshausen & Neumann, 2010), 54–61.

the rest of the often overlooked world that surrounds us. Seeing can lead us to know.

Poetic revelation occurs whenever something is uncovered and brought to light by the literary work of art. The poem is the incarnation of a certain way of seeing things, which has by now been identified as one that emphasizes their emotional coloring. More precisely, it is not that we lend false tints to an actually colorless world, but that we rely upon our own perceptive and attentive capacities, our affective and imaginative faculties, in experiencing things. "Reality is what we discern; but it is also what *we* discern," as a theorist of literary imagination has aptly noted,[16] and how we *say* that it is conditions how we *see* it. "If your everyday life seems poor," Rilke counsels, "don't blame it; blame yourself; admit to yourself that you are not enough of a poet to call forth its riches."[17] When fruit, jug, and flower are acknowledged in the song of the Orphic poet, they assume a reality in our inward experience, thus attaining a higher degree of objective reality, becoming "more truthful and more real than they otherwise might be,"[18] as their being is

16 Falck, *Myth, Truth, and Literature*, 66–67.

17 Letter of 17 February 1903 to Franz X. Kappus, in *Letters to a Young Poet*, trans. by Stephen Mitchell (New York: Vintage, 1986), 7–8. Cf. Jennifer Anna Gosetti-Ferencei, *Heidegger, Hölderlin, and the Subject of Poetic Language* (New York: Fordham University Press, 2004), 245: "*poetical cognition*," she claims, is "a grasp of something that is not, as in ordinary cognition, univocal and final," but that "rather remains open-endedly reverberant." Thomas Pfau comments upon how the poetic disclosure of truth involves finding an inexhaustible fecundity in things: "Superabundant Being," *Modern Theology* 35 (2019): 24.

18 Lou Andreas-Salomé, *You Alone Are Real to Me: Remembering Rainer Maria Rilke*, trans. by Angela von der Lippe (Rochester, NY: BOA Editions, 2003), 95. Merleau-Ponty also ascribes to art the power of "bringing truth into being." – *Phenomenology of Perception*, trans. by Colin Smith (New York: Routledge, 2002), xxiii.

disclosed. The most emphatic kind of poetic affirmation is wholehearted praise. "Praising, that's it! He was meant to praise," as Rilke writes of the archetypal Orphic poet in *Sonnets to Orpheus* I.7; for him, this above all is the poet's essential task: "endless affirmation and always more affirmation of existence."[19] His poetry therefore alludes to a state in which we celebrate everything that exists exactly as it is, perceived in the most radiant light – so that, as a result, life "is still enchanted and sacred,"[20] and felt to be worth living.

Of course, no affirmation of existence can be convincing unless it takes into account what is most horrifying. "Just as the artist may not choose what he wants to behold," or see only what he wants to see, he also "may not turn his gaze away from any form of existence."[21] This means that the poet must come to terms with all of the distressing features of human life, not least of which is the fragility and impermanence of all things. In a life of tragic suffering and loss, Rilke suggests (echoing the end of his Eighth *Duino Elegy*), we find ourselves forever taking leave, eventually departing from life itself. Rather than taking comfort in an evasion of this fact, or raging against it, Rilke attempts to make "an affirmation of the entire process that leads over and over again to death."[22]

19 Rilke, letter of 13 March 1920 to Rudolf Bodländer, in *The Poet's Guide to Life*, 59.

20 Paul Ricoeur, *Freedom and Nature*, trans. by Erazim Kohák (Evanston, IL: Northwestern University Press, 1966), 475.

21 Rilke, letter of 19 October 1907 to Clara Rilke, in *The Poet's Guide to Life*, 148–149. As Fischer writes, "To be sympathetic to the 'beautiful' or antipathetic toward the 'ugly' is to be partial in one's vision," so "the artist's way of seeing must acknowledge . . . the character of what would normally be repulsive or attractive," for only this "openness to all phenomena" allows for "a truthful revelation of things." See *The Poet as Phenomenologist*, 109–110.

22 Richard Detsch, *Rilke's Connections to Nietzsche* (Lanham, MD: University Press of America, 2003), 96. Cf. Donald Prater, *A Ring-*

He raises the question of whether we can ever be entirely at peace with our mortality: a poem (*Sonnets to Orpheus*, I.14) about "those now dead who fructify the earth" admits that we cannot expect anyone to be reconciled with his or her own demise.

> We are involved in flower, vine, and fruit:
> they speak not only the language of the year.
> Out of the dark appears a leafy shoot,
> its green suggestive of the jealous leer
>
> of those now dead who fructify the earth.
>
> [Wir gehen um mit Blume, Weinblatt, Frucht.
> Sie sprechen nicht die Sprache nur des Jahres.
> Aus Dunkel steigt ein buntes Offenbares
> und hat vielleicht den Glanz der Eifersucht
>
> der Toten an sich, die die Erde stärken.]

A few lines later, we are confronted with the question, "is it gladly done?" Or, on the contrary, is a plant that rises out of soil fertilized by those who have died "a clenched fist" raised in anger from underground? In light of our deep ambivalence about being finite, it is appropriate that the poem ends without offering a single determinate answer. The *Sonnets to Orpheus* do insist, however, on affirming "earthly and embodied" human existence "in the face of dissolution and death": here, no less than in Kierkegaard's pseudonymous *Fear and Trembling*, finitude is

ing Glass: The Life of Rainer Maria Rilke (Oxford: Oxford University Press, 1986), 353–354, on coming to terms with death instead of denying it.

"what it is all about."[23] The enormity of death must be accommodated within an affirmative stance. As he hints in the closing lines of the Fourth *Duino Elegy*, Rilke here in *Sonnets to Orpheus*, as in poems such as "Morgue" in the *Neue Gedichte*, impresses upon us how difficult it would be to comprehend our own mortality "and not to be driven mad."[24]

In another letter, Rilke considers that perhaps instead of seeking "consolation over a loss," we should "experience the peculiarity, the singularity, and the effects of this loss in our life," so that "its significance and weight" can inform our sense of what existence has meant for us.[25] Opting to regard the human predicament as meaningful whether or not it is a happy one, Rilke suggests that life can be affirmed whether or not it is worth affirming. To speak in praise of being, in other words, is not to claim that praise is unequivocally warranted. Always present in Rilke's poetry are the undertones of grief and lamentation, as the reader is "never given the impression that an optimist is speaking."[26] The reason for adopting a favorable attitude toward

23 Hannah Vandegrift Eldridge, *Lyric Orientations: Hölderlin, Rilke, and the Poetics of Community* (Ithaca, NY: Cornell University Press, 2015), 156–162; see also Søren Kierkegaard, *Fear and Trembling*, trans. by Sylvia Walsh (Cambridge: Cambridge University Press, 2006), 42.

24 From the penultimate line of the Fourth of the *Duino Elegies*, trans. by James D. Reid in *Being Here is Glorious: On Rilke, Poetry, and Philosophy* (Evanston, IN: Northwestern University Press, 2015), 99. Cf. Ernest Becker, *The Denial of Death* (New York: Free Press, 1973), 27: "I believe that those who speculate that a full apprehension of man's condition would drive him insane are right, quite literally right."

25 Letter of 6 January 1923 to Margot Sizzo, in *The Poet's Guide to Life*, 109.

26 Heinz F. Peters, *Rainer Maria Rilke: Masks and the Man* (Seattle: University of Washington Press, 1960), 177–178.

existence despite all of its sufferings and limitations is "not because happiness *is*," not because happiness exists, but "because being here is so much," and everything here

> apparently needs us, all those fugitive things that
> oddly penetrate us. Us, the most fugitive thing of all.[27]

> [uns scheinbar alles dasHiesige braucht, dieses Schwindende, das
> seltsam uns angeht. Uns, die Schwindendsten.]

Even a loss that brings a person tremendous emotional suffering is part of the meaning of his or her life, and for that reason its weight can be embraced and accepted no matter how devastating the loss may have been. Accordingly, in *Sonnets to Orpheus* I.4, Rilke writes: "Don't recoil from suffering." And, in II.21, he implores, "know that the whole tapestry is intended." Trust, in other words, that what you have experienced has not been at random or in vain – but that it has been *meant*, intended, as part of the significance of your particular being. Viewing your "deepest suffering" as meaningful (see II.29) is a plausible interpretation to make, even though the evidence of whether the whole tapestry is meant is indeterminate. A theme raised by other existential thinkers is that personal existence, what Kierkegaard calls "distinctiveness" or "peculiarity" ["*Eiendommelighed*"], matters in the ultimate scheme of things.

"Rejoicing knows," as Rilke writes in I.8, in the midst of a sonnet about the relations between lamentation and praise. There is a "'knowledge' that belongs to joy or praise," just as

27 From the Ninth of the *Duino Elegies*, trans. by James D. Reid in *Being Here is Glorious*, 121. See also Eldridge, *Lyric Orientations*, 31–32: "*Dasein* – or what Rilke will call *Hiersein*, being *here* – is all there is."

much as there is in sadness or sorrow.[28] "Joy," Rilke claims elsewhere, is something "more than happiness," because it is gratuitous: "happiness befalls people, happiness is fate, while people cause joy to bloom inside themselves."[29] With these words, he expresses the conviction that affirmation of existence must take the form of unconditional acceptance: this is an unjustifiable state of mind, not justified by particular evidence; nevertheless, some properties of the world would be lost on us in its absence. In the same manner that a congenitally blind person knows nothing about colors, the person who has not adopted the poet's "lyrical way of experiencing the world" is not fully aware of the meaning of things.[30] In order to discern significance in our environment, we must have an open, receptive attunement, what Rilke, like Heidegger, refers to as *Gelassenheit*. Nothing less is at stake in cultivating this disposition than "the birth of sense (or significance) itself," that is, the inward conditions that allow for the world's emergence and realization, that by virtue of which "beings come to be 'there' in the first place" in the "manifold ways" in which beings do

28 Eldridge, *Lyric Orientations*, 178–179.

29 Rilke, letter of 5 December 1914 to Marianne von Goldschmidt-Rothschild, in *The Poet's Guide to Life*, 175. According to Clément Rosset, the "central paradox of joy" is this: "Joy is an unconditional rejoicing for and with respect to existence, whereas existence is anything but joyful and heartening." See *Joyful Cruelty*, trans. by David F. Bell (New York: Oxford University Press, 1993), 15.

30 Wolfgang Leppmann, *Rilke: A Life*, trans. by Russell Stockman (New York: Fromm, 1984), 54–56. Cf. Priscilla Washburn Shaw, *Rilke, Valéry, and Yeats* (New Brunswick, NJ: Rutgers University Press, 1964), 76–77, on poetic "revelation" as "experiencing fully the reality and variety of the world." *Gelassenheit*, "a phenomenological or existential open-mindedness," is fruitfully discussed, with reference to relevant texts, by Fischer in *The Poet as Phenomenologist*, 102–112.

come to exist.[31] Rilke's emphasis throughout his sonnets is on *things felt*, not on feelings themselves in isolation from the world.

This explains the poet's continuing emphasis on "learning to see,"[32] and on striving to become more mindful and less oblivious toward concrete existence, to realizing "the truth of particular beings."[33] That is the goal, even when all that a literary artist can do is "to love the enigma," creating works out of "love which has been poured out over enigmas,"[34] and to bear witness to our failure to apprehend what it all means, as in *Sonnets to Orpheus*, I.19:

31 John Lysaker, *You Must Change Your Life: Poetry, Philosophy, and the Birth of Sense* (University Park, PA: Pennsylvania State University Press, 2002), 55 & 135–136. It would follow that springtime is not an event that takes place entirely apart from us; rather, it "requires the feelings appropriate to it" to "come into its own." – Konstantin Kolenda, "Immortality Revisited," *Philosophy and Literature* 4 (1980): 169. It is Rilke himself who spoke of having intended in his *New Poems* to capture things felt, not mere feelings. See, e.g., *New Poems*, trans. by Cadora, xxviii–xxix. On the difficulty of letting a thing be what it is, and thereby restoring ordinary *and* sacred meaning, see also Heidegger, *Poetry, Language, Thought*, 30–35. Cf. Julian Young, *Heidegger's Philosophy of Art* (Cambridge: Cambridge University Press, 2001), 143–147.

32 Rilke's path toward learning how to see is charted, e.g., throughout "The Florence Diary," in *Diaries of a Young Poet*, trans. by Edward Snow and Michael Winkler (New York: W. W. Norton & Company, 1997), 1–78. See David Kleinbard, *The Beginning of Terror* (New York: New York University Press, 1993), 23–47.

33 Heidegger, from "What Are Poets For?," 95–96. See also Lysaker, *You Must Change Your Life*, 34–37.

34 Rilke, "Worpswede," in *Where Silence Reigns: Selected Prose*, trans. by G. Craig Houston (New York: New Directions, 1978), 22. On this topic, and this passage, see also Reid, *Being Here is Glorious*, 52–54.

Suffering hasn't been fathomed,
nor love understood,
and that which death erases
remains no less obscure.

[Nicht sind die Leiden erkannt,
nicht ist die Liebe gelernt,
und was im Tod uns entfernt,

ist nicht entschleiert.]

Although his narrator Malte, in the *Notebooks*, ultimately fails to approach the world with a spirit of passionate acceptance, Rilke himself in another poem records the observation that this "world that is looked at so deeply / wants to flourish in love."[35] As another poet has pointed out, "the primary experience of perception" is shaped by "what the artist believes to be the qualitative nature of the things perceived."[36] How the poet sings of something affects how it is seen. When the Orphic poet "opens up to receive, in a flood of emotion, the being of the thing he sees," then he or she has arrived at the "way of seeing things" which is "the origin of poetry."[37]

35 From "Turning-Point," in *Selected Poetry of Rainer Maria Rilke*, trans. by Stephen Mitchell (New York: Vintage, 1989), 135. Malte's wish that he might be "learning to see" is found in *The Notebooks of Malte Laurids Brigge*, 14.

36 Kathleen Raine, *Defending Ancient Springs* (New York: Oxford University Press, 1967), 114. See also J. Glenn Gray, who urges us to "become aware that the poetic eye is capable of seeing as deeply . . . as the scientific eye." – "Poets and Thinkers," in *Phenomenology and Existentialism*, ed. by Edward N. Lee and Maurice Mandelbaum (Baltimore: Johns Hopkins University Press, 1967), 107.

37 J. Hillis Miller, *The Disappearance of God* (Urbana, IL: University

When I am in love with someone, I am capable of appreciating her best qualities, because these are enhanced in the light of my charitable gaze. The obligation that weighs on Rilke in the *Sonnets to Orpheus* is to extend this outlook so broadly that all of human existence is encompassed in a song of love, an anthem of unqualified praise. As we read in II.23,

> Anxiously we grapple for a hold —
> sometimes, we're too young for what is old
> and too old for that which never was.
>
> Still, it's only fair to praise, because:
> oh, nonetheless. We are the metal, and
> the sweet that looms and ripens on the branch.
>
> [Bang verlangen wir nach einem Halte,
> wir zu Jungen manchmal für das Alte
> und zu alt für das, was niemals war.
>
> Wir, gerecht nur, wo wir dennoch preisen,
> weil wir, ach, der Ast sind und das Eisen
> und das Süße reifender Gefahr.]

By now it ought to be clear that fundamental questions

of Illinois Press, 2000), 321. Making his point in relation to Gerard Manley Hopkins, he adds that in this type of apprehension "man is aware of the being of a thing, its beauty, its presence," thus seeing things "in terms of their existence." In this manner, "mortal beauty," although "dangerous," serves a purpose: it "keeps warm / Men's wits to the things that are," as Hopkins writes in an astonishingly Rilkean spirit. On "praise" as the poet's response to even "the nameless grays," see Rilke's untitled poem cited by Prater in *A Ringing Glass*, 351.

about the human condition can be gainfully explored in poetry. Others have already surmised that the existential philosopher's role may be to "describe the world in such a way that its meanings emerge," and that this job is perhaps best accomplished by more literary modes of writing.[38] The poet's appeal to emotion, and her attention to concrete particulars, cannot be seen as grounds for banishment from the ideal republic. According to Merleau-Ponty, even for philosophers it is not enough "to create or express an idea; they must also awaken the experiences which will make their idea take root in the consciousness of others."[39] If this is true, and if "axioms in philosophy are not axioms until they are proved upon our pulses," then poetic skill might be required in order for an author to bring a notion home to readers in a compelling and memorable way. This is especially the case if the idea to be brought home is an imperative that issues, as it were, from a classical sculpture of a headless god. An old piece of carved stone nonetheless confronts you, the viewer, with its vitality and its interrogative gaze: who are you? Are you yourself so real and intact that you are superior to a bit of broken, lifeless rock? The lack of a singular place from which a god regards you turns into a shocking feeling that God could therefore be

38 Mary Warnock, *Existentialism* (Oxford: Oxford University Press, 1970), 136. See also Colin Falck, *Myth, Truth, and Literature*, 60: "Lyric poetry might be thought of as the most essential of our linguistic modes of apprehension of reality." Cf. John Lysaker, *You Must Change Your Life*, 6–15. As Merleau-Ponty aptly notes, "everything we live and think has always several meanings." – *Phenomenology of Perception*, 196.

39 Maurice Merleau-Ponty, *Sense and Non-sense*, trans. by Hubert L. and Patricia Dreyfus (Evanston, IL: Northwestern University Press, 1964), 19. On how axioms need to be proved on our pulses, see *Letters of John Keats*, ed. by Robert Gittings (Oxford: Oxford University Press, 1970), 93.

looking from *everywhere*:[40] and this prompts the statement, "You must change your life" ["Du mußt dein Leben ändern"].

2

Yet there is more to be said about lyric poetry, beyond the fact that it can manifest an attitude or convey an idea. For if Rilke simply wanted to tell a tale or make an argument, then he might just as well be writing novels or essays instead of poems. Because he is composing poetry in a highly formal mode, a fixed form, Rilke is also calling our attention to the music of words, regardless of whatever else he is doing. Thus, his language is never merely a means to reaching an end outside the poem itself; so a flat, prosaic summary of a sonnet's narrative and propositional content would not exhaustively capture what is going on in the actual poem. In "Archaic Torso of Apollo," the arrival of that closing imperative, "You must change your life," has the force of a conclusion entailed by everything else that has come to voice in the sonnet. This includes its startling enjambments, caesuras, "collisions" and metrical "distortions" that impress upon the reader what a jarring encounter with the torso is being enacted here, one in which a perceptually felt

40 In this way, the sculpture in "Archaic Torso of Apollo" functions like the twelfth-century Romanesque church at Sæding in Denmark: "Without a spire pointing to any particular part of the vast Jutland sky," one can find "God's presence" looking down from anywhere in the "numinous skyscape." – Alastair Hannay, *Kierkegaard: Existence and Identity in a Post-Secular World* (London: Bloomsbury Academic, 2020), 48. Cf. Søren Kierkegaard, *Papers and Journals: A Selection*, 136: "The heath must be peculiarly suited to developing spiritual strength; here everything lies *naked* and *unveiled* before God." On the heath "one could truthfully say, 'Whither shall I flee from thy presence?'"

recognition impinges on the speaker.[41] The injunction to change one's life is not a dry intellectual proposition being dispassionately entertained, and this is made clear through the musical qualities of Rilke's lines as much as by *what* they say. Likewise in *Sonnets to Orpheus* II.1, where the mostly trochaic first line of tetrameter – "Breathing, you unseeable poem!" ["Atmen, du unsichtbares Gedicht!] – mimics and calls attention to the very rhythm of breath with which one utters it.[42] These features of poetry that deal with the sound of words are frequently not even considered in otherwise insightful readings of Rilke's sonnets – such as Heidegger's, to name one prominent case, although he is hardly alone in this.

Because both sound and sense demand our attention simultaneously, as readers we must attend to two aspects of a poem that *can* exist in tension with one another:[43] the sounds of words in a poem are distinct from their meanings. If a poet makes assertions or articulates theoretical views in verse, he or she cannot prevent

41 I quote Christian Jany, "'Das Anschauen ist eine so wunderbare Sache, von der wir noch so wenig wissen': Szenographien des Schauens beim mittleren Rilke," *Zeitschrift für Ästhetik und Allgemeine Kunstwissenschaft* 59 (2014): 156–160.

42 Cf. Claudia Röser, "Raumgewinn: Rhythmus und Raum in der Moderne: Rilkes Sonett 'Atmen'," *Zeitschrift für Kulturphilosophie* 7 (2013): 99–109. She finds spondaic meter here, as well as trochaic; this line also has an anapestic foot. Lysaker notes the near-irrelevance of "traditional poetic concerns" in Heidegger's interpretations: *You Must Change Your Life*, 21–28. See also Gosetti-Ferencei, *Heidegger, Hölderlin, and the Subject of Poetic Language*, 109: Heidegger gives "no consideration" to poetic form.

43 See Amittai F. Aviram, *Telling Rhythm: Body and Meaning in Poetry* (Ann Arbor, MI: University of Michigan Press, 1994), 47–50 & 56–57. On the "quite distinct" ways of thinking associated with poetry and philosophy, see John Koethe, "Thought and Poetry," *Midwest Studies in Philosophy* 25 (2001): 5.

"the attention given to following the ideas from competing with the attention that follows the song."[44] Yet, since words have meanings, even poetry that "privileges the phonic over the semantic function of language," as Rilke's does sometimes, can never become a "sheer play of signifiers" that displays rhyme but not reason; nor, on the other hand, can poetry consist in the defense of theses or the conveying of ready-made thoughts.[45] This means that the didactic poetry of Lucretius' *De Rerum Natura* is at odds with the nature of poetic language. It is therefore problematic to interpret Rilke's sonnets in a way that stresses only their conceptual content, which could be captured by a paraphrase. The music of poetry is actually relevant to its truth-revealing capacity, for reasons that I will explain further in a moment.

First, I should note that the duality of sense and sound poses a specific challenge for the translator of poetry. Since the primary goal of a poem is not to transmit information, it would not be sufficient to leap from one dictionary to another and construct a literal equivalent of the original poem's semantic content. Instead, one must remake the poem *as* a poem in the target or destination language. Insofar as the original poem is not merely saying things, but also *doing* things with words, a version of the poem in a different language should try to do the same kind of thing. So the translator of Rilke must strive to do justice to the sonic qualities of the original, not losing touch with Rilke's meaning or *how* it is meant and

44 Paul Valéry, *The Art of Poetry*, trans. by Denise Folliot (Princeton, NJ: Princeton University Press, 1958), 77–78. Cf. Michael Hamburger, *The Truth of Poetry* (New York: Harcourt Brace, 1970), 37–38: "Words can never be totally severed from the connection with ideas and meaning."

45 Véronique M. Fóti, *Heidegger and the Poets: Poiēsis/Sophia/Technē* (Atlantic Highlands, NJ: Humanities Press, 1992), 38.

said.[46] These twin exigencies give the translator poetic license to be a copyist and an original artist at the same time. Translating poems has a lot in common with writing poems, so the translator of poetry needs to be a poet while translating regardless of whether or not she also writes poetry of her own.[47]

By virtue of their conspicuous metrical structure, Rilke's sonnets serve as a reminder that poetry cannot be assimilated to any other genre of writing in which the sound of words does not command notice in the same way. This ought to be welcomed by those readers who love poetry for its own sake, rather than because a poem gives voice to feelings or beliefs they happen to endorse. "Most readers," Housman suggests, "when they think they are admiring poetry, are really admiring, not the poetry [itself] . . . but something else in it, which they like better than poetry."[48] Poems are made of words, and "words, above everything else, are, in poetry, sounds," as Stevens reminds us.[49] They

46 On "what is meant" and "the way of meaning it," see Walter Benjamin, "The Task of the Translator," in *Selected Writings: Volume One*, ed. by Michael W. Jennings and Marcus Bullock (Cambridge, MA: Harvard University Press, 1996), 257. The *what* and the *how* in relation to personal style, *haecceity*, are helpfully explicated by Fischer in *The Poet as Phenomenologist*, 46–59.

47 See Willis Barnstone, *The Poetics of Translation: History, Theory, Practice* (New Haven, CT: Yale University Press, 1993), 7–8 & 270–271.

48 A. E. Housman, *The Name and Nature of Poetry* (Cambridge: Cambridge University Press, 1933), 33–34. See also Aviram, *Telling Rhythm*, 114–121 & 228.

49 Wallace Stevens, from "The Noble Rider and the Sound of Words," in *The Necessary Angel: Essays on Reality and the Imagination* (New York: Vintage, 1951), 32. That poetry tends to aspire toward music as its "upper limit" is argued by Louis Zukofsky in "A Statement for Poetry." See *Prepositions: The Collected Critical Essays* (Middletown, CT: Wesleyan University Press, 2000), 19.

approach music as a kind of upper limit which they could not reach without giving up referential content and becoming disembodied ghosts. The cadences of words and phrases, the sound of vowels and staccato of consonants, and the rhyming within and at the end of the lines combine to highlight the physical texture of words – rather than only the paraphrasable meaning they convey. For instance, when Tennyson speaks of "myriads of rivulets hurrying through the lawn . . . and murmuring of innumerable bees," his theme is also demonstrably the musical aspect of language.[50] And much the same could be said of countless sequences in Rilke's sonnets – such as the first two lines of *Sonnets to Orpheus* II.5, whose assonances, rhythmic patterns, and other repetitions are evident in the original and also mirrored in the translation that follows:

> [Blumenmuskel, der der Anemone
> Wiesenmorgen nach und nach erschließt]

> Flower-flesh, unfolding bit by bit
> this anemone in the meadow dawn

In II.12, the alliterative echoes between "Ende" and "beginnt" ["mit Anfang oft schließt und mit Ende beginnt"] provide Rilke with an opportunity for the gnomic statement that creation "often ends at the start and begins at the end," an effect that transfers into English with the kindred words "end" and "begin." Although the translator's task is seldom so easy, it is important that any ostensible translation of a Rilke sonnet do something like what the original poem is doing – which means, in some way, duplicating or recreating its formal, musical aspect.

50 From "Come Down, O Maid," by Alfred Lord Tennyson, *The Princess*.

This is not irrelevant to the poem's truth-disclosing function, for there is an affective impression made on a listener by the pattern of sounds in a poem, however elusive it may be when we try to capture the significance of what has been impressed upon us, how a poem has moved us. It is not farfetched to concede that there must be a relation "between certain types of tonal gesturing and certain types of attitude."[51] For the sounds of a poem can intimate a state of mind over and above what thoughts it also contains. If only a part of the meaning of a poem can be conveyed by paraphrase, that is because "the poet is occupied with frontiers of consciousness beyond which words fail, though meanings still exist."[52] This is why it would be unwise "to dismiss [a] concern for attractive surfaces all too hastily as a form of aestheticism," lacking any deeper significance.[53] As Rilke himself states in a letter, rhyme is "the deity of very secret and very ancient coincidences."[54] The random fact that some words sound like others is an auspicious coincidence, from which many poetic discoveries can be gathered. Here are a few additional examples.

In *Sonnets to Orpheus* II.28, the rhyme between "Tanzfigur" and "Natur" prompts Rilke and his readers to view a "dance-figure" alongside "nature," as if the dancer's graceful motions are

51 Kenneth Burke, *The Philosophy of Literary Form* (New York: Vintage, 1957), 303. For Kathleen Raine, the music of a poem "communicates a meaning and a knowledge not of fact but of quality." *Defending Ancient Springs*, 175.

52 T. S. Eliot, "The Music of Poetry," in *On Poetry and Poets* (London: Faber and Faber, 1957), 30.

53 Paul de Man, *Allegories of Reading: Figural Language in Rousseau, Nietzsche, Rilke, and Proust* (New Haven, CT: Yale University Press, 1979), 22–23.

54 Letter of 23 March 1921 to Rolf von Ungern-Sternberg, in *The Poet's Guide to Life*, 130. Cf. J. Hillis Miller, *The Disappearance of God*, 279–280.

seemingly as natural as Nature herself. Yet it may be that this rhyme itself suggested the comparison to Rilke during his process of composing, just as the rhyme of "erfuhr" with "Natur" in *Sonnets to Orpheus* I.6 places the art of learning or knowing alongside what is natural. For it is by concentrating upon the technical demands of meter and rhyme that a poet who creates a sonnet becomes susceptible to thinking of potential formulations that would not have occurred to her otherwise. Lacking the liberty to jot down quickly the first things that come to mind, she is compelled to go beyond what she was already prepared to say. In this way, formal meter can be liberating since it provokes a poet to discover combinations of words that reveal something the poet did not already know.[55] Even if we take at face value Rilke's claims that the *Sonnets to Orpheus* were given to him as if dictated to his receptive faculties, and that his pen could hardly keep up with the pace of their disclosure,[56] the

55 See H. L. Hix, "Formal Experimentation and Poetic Discovery," in *As Easy as Lying: Essays on Poetry* (Silver Spring, MD: Etruscan Press, 2002), 50–56. This is why it is confused to insist that, if a poem uses rhyme, then "the rhyme must never lead to the introduction of unnecessary thought." *Thus to Revisit* by Ford Madox Ford (New York: Dutton, 1921), 206–207. Who decides in advance what is unnecessary? Cf. Donald Hall, *Goatfoot Milktongue Twinbird* (Ann Arbor, MI: University of Michigan Press, 1978), 117: "Technique can facilitate inspiration" because "concentration on technique can absorb the attention while unacknowledged material enters the language." An analogy between mystical experience and poetic composition is noted by Jennifer Anna Gosetti-Ferencei in *The Life of Imagination* (New York: Columbia University Press, 2018), 217–219.

56 As noted by, e.g., Thomas Martinec in "The *Sonnets to Orpheus*," in *The Cambridge Companion to Rilke*, ed. by Karen Leeder and Robert Vilain (Cambridge: Cambridge University Press, 2010), 95–96.

audible language still brought about genuine revelations, leading him to arrive at formulations that could not have been anticipated. In his engagement with the sonnet form, Rilke is less an author with a determinate "something to be said" and more of an artist with a technique that may bring something new to light.

Indeed, even when one of the *Sonnets to Orpheus* contains an aphoristic remark that lends itself more readily to being stated in prose, the form remains significant. Let's look again at two lines from I.19 (quoted above), a poem highlighted by Heidegger:

> [Nicht sind die Leiden erkannt,
> nicht ist die Liebe gelernt]
>
> Suffering hasn't been fathomed,
> nor love understood

As Heidegger comments in citing this poem, "The mystery of pain remains veiled. Love has not been learned."[57] This may capture most of what Rilke's lines mean, but the term *erkannt* sets up a rhyme with *Land* a few lines later, preparing the way for Rilke to envision the desecrated land made holy again, if at all, only by poetic song. He writes: "Einzig das Lied überm Land / heiligt und feiert." That is, "Song alone over the land / keeps holy and praises." The narrow trimeter lines in this poem permit Rilke to combine a succinct reflective observation with an ominous yet dimly hopeful vision of a place in need of profound renewal, a world no less fallen than the one that Eve willingly, if sadly, enters in the *New Poems* sonnet dedicated to her.

57 "What Are Poets For?," in *Poetry, Language, Thought*, 94–95.

And a musically compact line can express a truth that escapes being contained in a more prosaic utterance, especially when there is no plain statement to be made about the matter at hand. Just when we seem to have arrived at the boundary of the ineffable, our formal method enables us to say something rather than nothing, extending the range of what can be revealed through language.[58] Something like this may occur in the closing sestet of II.29, the final poem in the entire sequence:

> In this comprehensive night, become
> the junction where all senses intermix;
> be the truth of their odd rendezvous.
>
> And if the world has forgotten you,
> say this to the stable earth: I run.
> Tell the rushing water: I exist.
>
> [Sei in dieser Nacht aus Übermaß
> Zauberkraft am Kreuzweg deiner Sinne,
> ihrer seltsamen Begegnung Sinn.
>
> Und wenn dich das Irdische vergaß,
> zu der stillen Erde sag: Ich rinne.
> Zu dem raschen Wasser sprich: Ich bin.]

58 Christian Wiman discerns that "there are effects available to traditionally formal poems which aren't available to other poems," such as "an intensification of the uncertainty and even open-endedness that we normally associate with looser forms." – "An Idea of Order," in *After New Formalism: Poets on Form, Narrative, and Tradition*, ed. by Annie Finch (Ashland, OR: Story Line Press, 1999), 210.

Here, in the sestet of *Sonnets to Orpheus* II.29, the poet speaks in the imperative voice, using formal precision to delineate a specific attunement. It allows what had been indeterminate to be disclosed, as an unformulated thought takes definite shape.[59] From all of one's sufferings and the diverse confluence of one's influences, a distinctive identity comes to be affirmed as a singular event in the final lines, ending with an avowal of belief in oneself: *I exist.* An audibly rhythmic, precise formulation captures what a prosaic statement could not.

Rilke's sonnets are mainly shaped by the acoustic imagination. They are held together by patterns of assonance that echo off of one another even between the end rhymes that recur throughout the sequence. Their obsessive and repetitious rhythms serve to induce a state of heightened inwardness. And their musicality reminds us that, just as poetic language is "more than a vehicle for the transmission of axioms and concepts," so also rhythm is "more than a physiological motor. It is capable of registering . . . deep shocks of recognition."[60]

59 Here, I must take issue with Eugene Gendlin's way of characterizing the poet's implicit sense of the next line before it is written: see Gendlin, "How Philosophy Cannot Appeal to Experience, and How It Can," in *Language beyond Postmodernism*, ed. by David Michael Levin (Evanston, IL: Northwestern University Press, 1997), 17–18. The specificity of the *felt sense* described by Gendlin does inadequate justice to the indeterminacies of composition. See also Geoffrey Hill, *The Lords of Limit: Essays on Literature and Ideas* (Oxford: Oxford University Press, 1984), 117, on what a poet means before and after having found words to express his or her meaning.

60 Geoffrey Hill, *The Lords of Limit*, 87. See also P. Christopher Smith, "A Poem of Rilke," *Philosophy Today* 21 (1977): 254. Arthur Schopenhauer also points out that rhyme provides a sense of inevitability, reinforcing the conclusions at which a poem arrives. *The World as Will and Representation, Volume Two*, trans. by E. F. J. Payne (New York: Dover, 1966), 428–429.

These effects communicate intense feeling and conviction in a way that is only dissipated by the diffuse style of poems written in freer forms.[61] When the original poem is not merely saying things, but also *doing* things with the sounds of words, a version of the poem in a different language should do a similar kind of thing. This means that the translator of Rilke must strive to do justice to the sound of the original, not losing touch with either Rilke's meaning or *how* it is meant – namely, in variations of the sonnet form. Yet readers of some Rilke translations would be astounded to learn this. More often than not, Anglophone translators of Rilke have presumed that readers need not experience anything like the texture and form of the original sonnets, and that these can be safely omitted.

For instance, William Gass and Robert Bly are contemporary authors who have ventured to translate some of the *Sonnets to Orpheus* while commenting on how the poems ought to be translated. Not only do both of them make little use of those features of the sonnets that make them qualify *as* sonnets – namely, their patterns of rhyme and meter – but they also volunteer their own scornful and dismissive views of metrical form.

61 The same point is made by Louis Mackey in *Kierkegaard: A Kind of Poet* (Philadelphia: University of Pennsylvania Press, 1971), 267. Samuel Taylor Coleridge calls for "a more than usual state of emotion" to be combined in a poet with "more than usual order": see *Biographia Literaria*, ed. by Nigel Leak (London: Everyman, 1997), 185. See also Anthony Storr, *Music and the Mind* (New York: Ballantine Books, 1992), 103: "Those who are especially threatened by disorder are those most strongly motivated to discover order." Timothy Steele makes a similar point during an interview with William Baer: see *The Formalist* 14 (2003): 28–29. Henry Hart speaks of "pattern[ing] chaotic energies" or "patterning chaos" in *The Poetry of Geoffrey Hill* (Carbondale, IL: Southern Illinois University Press, 1986), 24 & 195.

Gass takes the second poem (I.2) and distorts its rhymed pentameter sestet into seven irregular lines of free verse, ranging from five to twelve syllables in length, then contends that he has rendered the poem "as the poet wrote it."[62] Bly, who likewise scoffs at formal poetry generally and at the sonnet especially, expands the phrase *Gesang ist Dasein* from *Sonnets to Orpheus* I.3 from three words to seven, turning it from a compact, suggestive aphorism into an ordinary-language paraphrase: "to write poetry is to be alive."[63] The major problem with this is that it captures, at best, only one of the plurality of meanings inherent in "Song is existence." Yet "the greater ambiguity of poetic language," as opposed to conceptual explanation, is not only to its detriment:[64] when Rilke's richly ambiguous poem is replaced by Bly's version (which is more of an interpretation than a translation), it does not get helpfully clarified but instead becomes less than it is. "Song is being" signifies so much more than simply "to write poetry is to be alive." As this example illustrates, poetry composed in an intricate form must be handled in a way that avoids the heresy of paraphrase by replacing the poem with a summary of what it means, and focusing only on what the poem is

62 William H. Gass, *Reading Rilke: Reflections on the Problems of Translation* (New York: Knopf, 1999), 84–85. Other snide remarks on the sonnet form can be found on page 52. For some of his cheap shots at Rilke's "alleged ideas," mere "emotions" and "moods" that are not "philosophical," see pages 32–33 and 110. As Coetzee notes, Gass conveys the patronizing attitude that, "compared with William Gass, Rilke was a bit of a fool, a bit of a booby." – J. M. Coetzee, *Stranger Shores: Literary Essays* (New York: Penguin, 2002), 64–65.

63 *Selected Poems of Rainer Maria Rilke,* trans. by Robert Bly (New York: Harper & Row, 1981), 198–199.

64 Fischer, *The Poet as Phenomenologist*, 226–227; see also Eliot, *On Poetry and Poets*, 22.

"about."[65] Rilke's poems are not transparently written on *topics* as newspaper articles are expected to be. Moreover, the rhythms of a sonnet involve the listener's body when he or she recites or hears the poem. Compared to the musical iambs of the original sonnet, the phrase "to write poetry is to be alive" sounds remarkably flat. Another of Rilke's translators, Willis Barnstone, is so bold as to say that, "if one disapproves of rhyme in poetry," then perhaps "one should not translate poems that rhyme."[66] Nor should someone who believes that "faith in *anything* is misplaced" regard himself as qualified to convey the spirit of Rilke's words,[67] given the confidence shown by the author of *Sonnets to Orpheus* in the sacred task of the literary artist.

3

For Rilke, Orpheus is the archetypal poet, the incarnation of the creative impulse, and the thinker who teaches us how to face life and death with wisdom and courage. The poet's own favorite sonnet, which he described as the "most valid" poem in the

65 On "the heresy of paraphrase," see Cleanth Brooks, *The Well Wrought Urn* (New York: Harcourt Brace, 1947), 192–214. Roman Ingarden notes that there can be no entirely faithful translation of a lyric poem in *The Cognition of the Literary Work of Art*, trans. by Ruth Ann Crowley and Kenneth R. Olson (Evanston, IL: Northwestern University Press, 1973), 156.

66 Barnstone, "Preferences in Translating Poetry," in *Translation*, ed. by William Frawley (Newark, DE: University of Delaware Press, 1984), 50.

67 Don Paterson, *Orpheus* (London: Faber & Faber, 2006), 79. Yet there is something admirable in this irreverent spirit. Rilke translators might do well to follow Paterson, who "can read a very little of a few languages," and bear in mind that, "in the translation of poetry, even a very *good* acquaintance with the source language is no guarantee of anything at all." – *Orpheus*, 81–82.

sequence and as the one that "contains all the rest," is the poem (II.13) that opens with the directive, "Be ahead of all parting," and which includes this appeal:

> Amid these fading and decaying things,
> be the glass that rings out as it's breaking.
> [Hier, unter Schwindenden, sei, im Reiche der Neige,
> sei ein klingendes Glas, das sich im Klang schon zerschlug.]

It is a sonnet of passionate affirmation, a meditation on human mortality and meaning. Life as a whole is presented as a complex episode of departure, always charged with the prospect of loss. In this predicament, nothing can suffice to provide us with abiding fulfillment – yet we are asked to be grateful toward the source of our being, to embrace the ambiguous mystery of our existence. The attitude endorsed by Rilke here is one of unconditional acceptance toward an unknown ground of being.[68] In its closing lines, the sonnet ends with a formal resolution that leaves room for uncertainty; by doing so, it refuses to give the illusion of having answered an irresolvable question that can only be faced in fear and trembling.

As opposed to the attitude of technological dominance,

68 On the inescapable, irresolvable nature of existential problems, see Else Buddeberg, *Denken und Dichten des Seins: Heidegger/Rilke* (Stuttgart: J. B. Metzlersche Verlagsbuchhandlung, 1956), 47–49. Maurice Blanchot comments upon how Rilke elevates unsureness into "the resolution of an exact formulation." See *The Space of Literature*, trans. by Ann Smock (Lincoln, NE: University of Nebraska Press, 1982), 144. The possibility of resolving intellectual and emotional perplexities in a sonnet as opposed to another literary form is examined by Paul Oppenheimer in *The Birth of the Modern Mind: Self, Consciousness, and the Invention of the Sonnet* (New York: Oxford University Press, 1989), 3–4.

the willful self-assertion of one's purposes onto the world, Rilke offers an alternative ideal that is enacted in his sonnets. Just as he opts to work with the very recalcitrance of language, the poet also accepts the finite restrictions of the actual world as the space within which he must live. Receptivity in creating replaces the notion of forcing the world into conformity with one's will, and being happy only insofar as it accords with how we want it to be. We do not *assign* significance to the things around us, but rather *allow* them to be significant.[69] A genuine poet is moved not only when, for instance, she recollects in tranquillity a moment of emotion, but also when she succeeds at being "open and receptive" (see the end of *Sonnets to Orpheus* II.5). At the heart of Rilke's idea of receptivity is what I have portrayed as an affirmative embrace of concrete life in this world as meaningful and valuable, with a clear vision of "the many reasons to be dissatisfied, perplexed, and skeptical."[70]

69 "Letting things be relevant" is discussed by Heidegger in *Being and Time*, trans. by Joan Stambaugh (Albany, NY: SUNY Press, 1996), § 69. It becomes a more pronounced theme in his later work, as is noted by Gosetti-Ferencei in *Heidegger, Hölderlin, and the Subject of Poetic Language*, 10. Due to care, or – one might also say – to love, a significant world comes to light: see also Kip Wilson, *Force and Love in the Works of Rainer Maria Rilke: Heroic Life Attitudes and the Acceptance of Defeat and Suffering as Complementary Parts* (Frankfurt am Main: Peter Lang, 1999), 99. On how our personhood is shaped by the ways in which we have opened ourselves to a love of "true being," including encounters with works of art, see Lambert Zuidervaart, *Artistic Truth* (Cambridge: Cambridge University Press, 2004), 39–41.

70 Reid, *Being Here is Glorious*, 9. Cf. Kathleen L. Komar, *Transcending Angels* (Lincoln, NE: University of Nebraska Press, 1987), 184: "The joy of the sonnets can arise only after the lamentations of the *Elegies*." Gerald L. Bruns makes the provocative statement that the closing lines of *Sonnets to Orpheus* I.3 capture "the whole point"

Realized in *Sonnets to Orpheus* is his anti-nihilistic vision of reality, not as bare matter awaiting the imposition of meaning, but as disclosing its meaning to the observer who is suitably attentive and receptive. "Song, as you remind us, isn't longing, / not a plea for some end to be achieved" (I.3). Rather, he proposes:

> Song is existence – easy for a god,
> but when do *we* exist? And when does *he*
>
> circle the earth and stars around our being?
> Not when you're young and in love, even if
> your voice erupts in tongues at such a time.
>
> Learn to forget that song – it will decline.
> True singing needs another way to breathe.
> A "nothing" breath. A gust of god. A wind.
>
> [Gesang ist Dasein. Für den Gott ein Leichtes.
> Wann aber *sind* wir? Und wann wendet *er*
>
> an unser Sein die Erde und die Sterne?
> Dies *ists* nicht, Jüngling, daß du liebst, wenn auch
> die Stimme dann den Mund dir aufstößt, – lerne
>
> vergessen, daß du aufsangst. Das verrinnt.
> In Wahrheit singen, ist ein andrer Hauch.
> Ein Hauch um nichts. Ein Wehn im Gott. Ein Wind.]

of poetry. See *Heidegger's Estrangements: Language, Truth, and Poetry in the Later Writings* (New Haven, CT: Yale University Press, 1989), 155–156.

4

In this collection, the complete *Sonnets to Orpheus* are preceded by a set of "middle" poems, that is, sixteen sonnets from the *Neue Gedichte*, which were composed over a decade before the *Sonette an Orpheus* and signify the emergence of Rilke's mature style. With the exception of placing "Archaic Torso of Apollo" at the front due to its status as the most widely admired sonnet in the *New Poems*, I have left these in the order in which Rilke decided they would appear. Then, at the very end, an extremely rare late sonnet in French serves as a coda for the book. Without abandoning his native German language, the longtime Francophile Rilke wrote numerous poems in French during the last few years of his life. Most of these are quite short, many of the "longer" ones are *thirteen* lines long, and in this phase of Rilke's work the sonnet form has been *almost* entirely abandoned. This lone poem, "To Speak a Flower," is like other Rilkean sonnets from "The Marble Cart" through so many of the Orpheus poems – in the sense that it invites us to construe it as, among other things, an elegant analogy for the process of poetic composition. Ending with the tactful understatement that the poet "very well might speak a flower," it leaves us likely to agree with this modest claim: yes, he just might.

Die Sonette von Rainer Maria Rilke

Aus *Neue Gedichte*

The Sonnets of Rainer Maria Rilke

from *New Poems*

Archaïscher Torso Apollos

Wir kannten nicht sein unerhörtes Haupt,
darin die Augenäpfel reiften. Aber
sein Torso glüht noch wie ein Kandelaber,
in dem sein Schauen, nur zurückgeschraubt,

sich hält und glänzt. Sonst könnte nicht der Bug
der Brust dich blenden, und im leisen Drehen
der Lenden könnte nicht ein Lächeln gehen
zu jener Mitte, die die Zeugung trug.

Sonst stünde dieser Stein entstellt und kurz
unter der Schultern durchsichtigem Sturz
und flimmerte nicht so wie Raubtierfelle;

und bräche nicht aus allen seinen Rändern
aus wie ein Stern: denn da ist keine Stelle,
die dich nicht sieht. Du mußt dein Leben ändern.

Archaic Torso of Apollo

We cannot grasp his once envisioned head,
his lively eyesight lit with the divine:
yet in his body, this is always brilliant.
His look still blazes forth as in the fiery,

steady glow of gas-lamps. Otherwise,
you wouldn't be bedazzled, to the verge
of going blind, by a chest that swells above
the smiling pelvis with its yearning urges.

Or else this stone would seem defaced and short
beneath its shoulders and transparent eyes –
not glistening like a wild creature's face.

Nor would its look from every edge burst forth
with starlight streaming. For there is no place
that fails to see you. You must change your life.

Der Tod des Dichters

Er lag. Sein aufgestelltes Antlitz war
bleich und verweigernd in den steilen Kissen,
seitdem die Welt und dieses von-ihr-Wissen,
von seinen Sinnen abgerissen,
zurückfiel an das teilnahmslose Jahr.

Die, so ihn leben sahen, wußten nicht,
wie sehr er Eines war mit allem diesen;
denn Dieses: diese Tiefen, diese Wiesen
und diese Wasser *waren* sein Gesicht.

O sein Gesicht war diese ganze Weite,
die jetzt noch zu ihm will und um ihn wirbt;
und seine Maske, die nun bang verstirbt,
ist zart und offen wie die Innenseite
von einer Frucht, die an der Luft verdirbt.

The Death of the Poet

He lay there, with his pale face vertical
on pillows, as in a gesture of refusing,
now that this world and what he knew of her
got ripped apart from sensory discernment
and fell back on the unresponsive year.

Those who glimpsed him living did not grasp
how much he was at one with all of this:
for these deep canyons, open meadows, and
those running *waters* also, fixed his visage.

His face is stretched along across the taut
breadth that searched for him, as if to seduce,
whereas his mask expresses frightful thoughts.
It's tender, like the inside of a fruit
split open to the unsafe air and ruined.

Morgue

Da liegen sie bereit, als ob es gälte,
nachträglich eine Handlung zu erfinden,
die mit einander und mit dieser Kälte
sie zu versöhnen weiß und zu verbinden;

denn das ist alles noch wie ohne Schluß.
Wasfür ein Name hätte in den Taschen
sich finden sollen? An dem Überdruß
um ihren Mund hat man herumgewaschen:

er ging nicht ab; er wurde nur ganz rein.
Die Bärte stehen, noch ein wenig härter,
doch ordentlicher im Geschmack der Wärter,

nur um die Gaffenden nicht anzuwidern.
Die Augen haben hinter ihren Lidern
sich umgewandt und schauen jetzt hinein.

Morgue

There they lie prepared, as if to take
some strategic action after the fact
that would reconcile them with this cold,
uniting them with one another at last –

for everything remains without conclusion.
What kind of name could possibly have been
within those pockets? Someone washed around
their mouths, and yet the look of weariness

could not be scrubbed off, only sanitized.
The beards grow stiff, according to the taste
of those funeral guards, in order not

to repulse the passersby who gawk.
Hidden behind closed lids, the eyes have turned
away from waking worlds and look inside.

Blaue Hortensie

So wie das letzte Grün in Farbentiegeln
sind diese Blätter, trocken, stumpf und rauh,
hinter den Blütendolden, die ein Blau
nicht auf sich tragen, nur von ferne spiegeln.

Sie spiegeln es verweint und ungenau,
als wollten sie es wiederum verlieren,
und wie in alten blauen Briefpapieren
ist Gelb in ihnen, Violett und Grau;

Verwaschnes wie an einer Kinderschürze,
Nichtmehrgetragnes, dem nichts mehr geschieht:
wie fühlt man eines kleinen Lebens Kürze.

Doch plötzlich scheint das Blau sich zu verneuen
in einer von den Dolden, und man sieht
ein rührend Blaues sich vor Grünem freuen.

Blue Hydrangea

Just as the green paint leaves a final tint
in the pan, the dry leaves, dull and rough,
retain a trace of blue – as if to hint
that what at last abides here is enough.

Reflecting their sad ambiguities,
like faces reconciled to fading mirth,
they settle onto pages with the ease
of yellow animating grayish-purple.

The final shade of light on childish smocks
that have been set aside, no longer used,
reveals an ending, like our fleeting span.

But all at once the blue appears renewed;
a blossom, all alone, discloses broad
bright sky ascending over verdant grass.

Der Marmor-Karren

Auf Pferde, sieben ziehende, verteilt,
verwandelt Niebewegtes sich in Schritte;
denn was hochmütig in des Marmors Mitte
an Alter, Widerstand und All verweilt,

das zeigt sich unter Menschen. Siehe, nicht
unkenntlich, unter irgend einem Namen,
nein: wie der Held das Drängen in den Dramen
erst sichtbar macht und plötzlich unterbricht:

so kommt es durch den stauenden Verlauf
des Tages, kommt in seinem ganzen Staate,
als ob ein großer Triumphator nahte

langsam zuletzt; und langsam vor ihm her
Gefangene, von seiner Schwere schwer.
Und naht noch immer und hält alles auf.

The Marble Cart

The unyielding, its weight sustained
by seven horses, gets forced into motion;
as haughty as the All, the old marble
reflects us human beings in its inertia:

we, the sculptors. Undeniably,
as when, in a dramatic spectacle,
a character, known by whatever name,
disrupts the action at some interval

abruptly: thus, the wagon ushers on
through the congestion like a regiment,
with all its pomp and circumstance parading

slowly. As the prisoners who labor
forward with their burden rumble nearer,
all else is prompted suddenly to stop.

Römische Fontäne

Zwei Becken, eins das andre übersteigend
aus einem alten runden Marmorrand,
und aus dem oberen Wasser leis sich neigend
zum Wasser, welches unten wartend stand,

dem leise redenden entgegenschweigend
und heimlich, gleichsam in der hohlen Hand,
ihm Himmel hinter Grün und Dunkel zeigend
wie einen unbekannten Gegenstand;

sich selber ruhig in der schönen Schale
verbreitend ohne Heimweh, Kreis aus Kreis,
nur manchmal träumerisch und tropfenweis

sich niederlassend an den Moosbehängen
zum letzten Spiegel, der sein Becken leis
von unten lächeln macht mit Übergängen.

Roman Fountain

Two basins, one overhanging the other,
each with an ancient marble rim, convey
water from the higher to the lower,
bending gently downward, with a way

of murmuring so quietly, as if
to speak of secrets written in the hand.
Beyond it all, green darkness fills the sky,
like a thing we cannot understand.

Circle out of circle, without nostalgia,
the water spreads within the splendid bowl;
when it's one at a time that droplets trickle

over the mossy contours, changing form
repeatedly, reaching the final mirror,
the lower basin smiles at every ripple.

Der Tod der Geliebten

Er wußte nur vom Tod was alle wissen:
daß er uns nimmt und in das Stumme stößt.
Als aber sie, nicht von ihm fortgerissen,
nein, leis aus seinen Augen ausgelöst,

hinüberglitt zu unbekannten Schatten,
und als er fühlte, daß sie drüben nun
wie einen Mond ihr Mädchenlächeln hatten
und ihre Weise wohlzutun:

da wurden ihm die Toten so bekannt,
als wäre er durch sie mit einem jeden
ganz nah verwandt; er ließ die andern reden

und glaubte nicht und nannte jenes Land
das gutgelegene, das immersüße –
Und tastete es ab für ihre Füße.

The Death of the Beloved

He knew of death what everyone can grasp:
that it makes us mute and takes us away.
Yet when she was – not torn apart from him,
but gently separated from his gaze –

she drifted over toward unknown shadows.
And when he felt that those who were over there
now owned the brightness of her youthful smile,
like a moon, and her distinctive flair,

then the dead became like family
because through them he was related to her;
he let them speak, but he did not believe.

He named that country's fragrance forever
sweet, its place well-situated, and
explored its many spaces for her feet.

Eine Sibylle

Einst, vor Zeiten, nannte man sie alt.
Doch sie blieb und kam dieselbe Straße
täglich. Und man änderte die Maße,
und man zählte sie wie einen Wald

nach Jahrhunderten. Sie aber stand
jeden Abend auf derselben Stelle,
schwarz wie eine alte Citadelle
hoch und hohl und ausgebrannt;

von den Worten, die sich unbewacht
wider ihren Willen in ihr mehrten,
immerfort umschrieen und umflogen,
während die schon wieder heimgekehrten
dunkel unter ihren Augenbogen
saßen, fertig für die Nacht.

A Sibyl

Once upon a time, they called her old.
But she remained and walked along the same
street daily. Then they sought to rearrange
the count, and tell her age more like a forest,

in centuries. Yet every evening she
kept standing there, as black as any ancient
castle – monumental, towering,
empty as a shell, burnt-out, and ageless.

Words flew unguardedly, against her will,
and some continued, as it were, to squawk
unendingly – even as their flight

began to bend back home. The ones that did
already rest in friendly roosts were calm,
darkling beneath her brows, prepared for night.

Der Alchimist

Seltsam verlächelnd schob der Laborant
den Kolben fort, der halbberuhigt rauchte.
Er wußte jetzt, was er noch brauchte,
damit der sehr erlauchte Gegenstand

da drin entstände. Zeiten brauchte er,
Jahrtausende für sich und diese Birne
in der es brodelte; im Hirn Gestirne
und im Bewußtsein mindestens das Meer.

Das Ungeheuere, das er gewollt,
er ließ es los in dieser Nacht. Es kehrte
zurück zu Gott und in sein altes Maß;

er aber, lallend wie ein Trunkenbold,
lag über dem Geheimfach und begehrte
den Brocken Gold, den er besaß.

The Alchemist

With a curious smile, the lab technician
pushed away the half-calm, smoking flask.
He understood what else was needed now
to create the treasured element at last

within this pear-shaped glass. He needed time,
millennia for him to let it seethe
and foam; he needed stars within his brain,
an ocean in his consciousness at least.

That night, the man let loose the monster he
himself had willed to be. So it returned
to God and to its ancient magnitude;

but, talking gibberish like any drunkard,
he covered the unknown receptacle
and coveted his chunk of gold anew.

Eva

Einfach steht sie an der Kathedrale
großem Aufstieg, nah der Fensterrose,
mit dem Apfel in der Apfelpose,
schuldlos-schuldig ein für alle Male

an dem Wachsenden, das sie gebar,
seit sie aus dem Kreis der Ewigkeiten
liebend fortging, um sich durchzustreiten
durch die Erde, wie ein junges Jahr.

Ach, sie hätte gern in jenem Land
noch ein wenig weilen mögen, achtend
auf der Tiere Eintracht und Verstand.

Doch da sie den Mann entschlossen fand,
ging sie mit ihm, nach dem Tode trachtend;
und sie hatte Gott noch kaum gekannt.

Eve

Atop the steep cathedral, gracefully
she stands beside the window tinted rose,
forever in her guilty innocence
holding the apple in the apple pose,

involved in all the growing she gave birth
to, since she lovingly left the sphere
of eternity to skirmish through
the earth, as if within an infant year.

Oh, she would have liked to linger there,
in that land, to live in unity
and understanding with the animals.

Yet, because she noticed that the man
insisted, she complied, accepting death,
departing from a God she hardly knew.

Fremde Familie

So wie der Staub, der irgendwie beginnt
und nirgends ist, zu unerklärtem Zwecke
an einem leeren Morgen in der Ecke
in die man sieht, ganz rasch zu Grau gerinnt,

so bildeten sie sich, wer weiß aus was,
im letzten Augenblick vor deinen Schritten
und waren etwas Ungewisses mitten
im nassen Niederschlag der Gasse, das

nach dir verlangte. Oder nicht nach dir.
Denn eine Stimme, wie vom vorigen Jahr,
sang dich zwar an und blieb doch ein Geweine;
und eine Hand, die wie geliehen war,
kam zwar hervor und nahm doch nicht die deine.
Wer kommt denn noch? Wen meinen diese vier?

Unfamiliar Family

Just like the dust that randomly shows up
out of nowhere, inexplicably,
on an empty morning, in a corner,
quickly turning gray for all to see,

so, out of who knows where, they group themselves
right where you are walking at this instant –
in the street they form a thing uncertain,
like the raindrops drifting in a windstorm,

clamoring for you. Or maybe not.
Because a voice, one from another year,
cried out to you and lingered like a cry;

and a hand reached out, but did not seize
your own, as if being offered to lend.
Who are these four? What do they want from me?

Römische Campagna

Aus der vollgestellten Stadt, die lieber
schliefe, träumend von den hohen Thermen,
geht der grade Gräberweg ins Fieber;
und die Fenster in den letzten Fermen

sehn ihm nach mit einem bösen Blick.
Und er hat sie immer im Genick,
wenn er hingeht, rechts und links zerstörend,
bis er draußen atemlos beschwörend

seine Leere zu den Himmeln hebt,
hastig um sich schauend, ob ihn keine
Fenster treffen. Während er den weiten

Aquädukten zuwinkt herzuschreiten,
geben ihm die Himmel für die seine
ihre Leere, die ihn überlebt.

Roman Plains

From the crowded city that would prefer
to sleep, and dream of lofty thermal baths,
the road of graves goes straight into a fever
and, looking out the windows of the last

farms, somebody watches with an evil
stare. It feels this on the back of its neck
as it heads forward, conjuring, destructive,
arriving outside when it's out of breath.

Its emptiness arises to the sky;
it casts around a quick glance to make sure
there is nobody looking, beckoning

toward those big aqueducts. Up high,
the heavens trade their emptiness for its
own, knowing that it will endure.

Spätherbst in Venedig

Nun treibt die Stadt schon nicht mehr wie ein Köder,
der alle aufgetauchten Tage fängt.
Die gläsernen Paläste klingen spröder
an deinen Blick. Und aus den Gärten hängt

der Sommer wie ein Haufen Marionetten
kopfüber, müde, umgebracht.
Aber vom Grund aus alten Waldskeletten
steigt Willen auf: als sollte über Nacht

der General des Meeres die Galeeren
verdoppeln in dem wachen Arsenal,
um schon die nächste Morgenluft zu teeren

mit einer Flotte, welche ruderschlagend
sich drängt und jäh, mit allen Flaggen tagend,
den großen Wind hat, strahlend und fatal.

Late Autumn in Venice

Now the city is no longer drifting
like a bait that catches every parting
day. Glass palaces seem brittler
as you look. The summer hangs from gardens

upside down, a set of marionettes
worn out and extinguished. From the ground,
volition dawns out of old skeletons
– as if the overseer of seas somehow,

overnight, had multiplied by two
the galleys in the wakeful arsenal,
to cover with tar the early morning air

with a strong armada that forces its oars
and pushes forward suddenly, all flags
aloft in the strong wind, invincible.

Dame vor dem Spiegel

Wie in einem Schlaftrunk Spezerein
löst sie leise in dem flüssigklaren
Spiegel ihr ermüdetes Gebaren;
und sie tut ihr Lächeln ganz hinein.

Und sie wartet, daß die Flüssigkeit
davon steigt; dann gießt sie ihre Haare
in den Spiegel und, die wunderbare
Schulter hebend aus dem Abendkleid,

trinkt sie still aus ihrem Bild. Sie trinkt,
was ein Liebender imn Taumel tränke,
prüfend, voller Mißtraun; und sie winkt

erst der Zofe, wenn sie auf dem Grunde
ihres Spiegels Lichter findet, Schränke
und das Trübe einer späten Stunde.

Lady Facing a Mirror

As into a sleeping potion spices are
stirred, she relinquishes her tired
demeanor, gently letting it melt into
the liquid mirror; finally, her smile

gets poured in. Waiting for its liquidness
to rise up, she begins to spill her hair
into the mirror, drinking from this image,
leaning out of her evening gown a bare,

glorious shoulder. What a frenzied lover
might consume filled with suspicion, she
gently imbibes; and does not call her maid

until she has found candles, cabinets,
and, at the very basis of her mirror,
this late hour's morose obscurity.

Die Flamingos

In Spiegelbildern wie von Fragonard
ist doch von ihrem Weiß und ihrer Röte
nicht mehr gegeben, als dir einer böte,
wenn er von seiner Freundin sagt: sie war

noch sanft von Schlaf. Denn steigen sie ins Grüne
und stehn, auf rosa Stielen leicht gedreht,
beisammen, blühend, wie in einem Beet,
verführen sie verführender als Phryne

sich selber; bis sie ihres Auges Bleiche
hinhalsend bergen in der eignen Weiche,
in welcher Schwarz und Fruchtrot sich versteckt.

Auf einmal kreischt ein Neid durch die Volière;
sie aber haben sich erstaunt gestreckt
und schreiten einzeln ins Imaginäre.

The Flamingos

In Fragonard's reflected images,
no more of their white and red is offered
than if some other person were to say
about his beloved woman: she was softly

sleeping. Within the greenery they climb
and rotate on their stems, pink, blossoming
together as if in a flower bed,
seducing even more seductively

than Phyrne; they hide the color of their eyes
in their own downy softness, which conceals
unseen rosy fruit tints mixed with pitch.

A shriek of envy leaves the aviary
suddenly – but they, surprised, just stretch
and step, one by one, into the imaginary.

Persisches Heliotrop

Es könnte sein, daß dir der Rose Lob
zu laut erscheint für deine Freundin: Nimm
das schön gestickte Kraut und überstimm
mit dringend flüsterndem Heliotrop

den Bülbül, der an ihren Lieblingsplätzen
sie schreiend preist und sie nicht kennt.
Denn sieh: wie süße Worte nachts in Sätzen
beisammenstehn ganz dicht, durch nichts getrennt,
aus der Vokale wachem Violett
hindüftend durch das stille Himmelbett – :

so schließen sich vor dem gesteppten Laube
deutliche Sterne zu der seidnen Traube
und mischen, daß sie fast davon verschwimmt,
die Stille mit Vanille und mit Zimmt.

Persian Heliotrope

It may be that the rose's flattery
would seem too garish for your lady friend;
so allow the heliotrope's urgent whisper,
its beautiful embroidery, to win

out over even the loudest of songbirds,
who praises what it scarcely knows or sees
in her loved places. Note how sweet words stand
together nightly, with nothing in between,
and how the violet of the wakeful vowels
lends fragrance to the sleeping canopy.

Above the quilted alcove, distinct stars
combine in silky bunches as they mix,
not quite blurring midnight and its silence
with minglings of vanilla and cinnamon.

Sonette an Orpheus

Sonnets to Orpheus

I.1

Da stieg ein Baum. O reine Übersteigung!
O Orpheus singt! O hoher Baum im Ohr!
Und alles schwieg. Doch selbst in der Verschweigung
ging neuer Anfang, Wink und Wandlung vor.

Tiere aus Stille drangen aus dem klaren
gelösten Wald von Lager und Genist;
und da ergab sich, daß sie nicht aus List
und nicht aus Angst in sich so leise waren,

sondern aus Hören. Brüllen, Schrei, Geröhr
schien klein in ihren Herzen. Und wo eben
kaum eine Hütte war, dies zu empfangen,

ein Unterschlupf aus dunkelstem Verlangen
mit einem Zugang, dessen Pfosten beben, –
da schufst du ihnen Tempel im Gehör.

I.1

A tree rose up. Oh zenith of arising!
Sing, Orpheus! The highest in the ear!
And all was still. Yet, even in the silence,
new things proceeded; hints of change appeared.

Out of the quiet, creatures came to light,
emerging from both earth and wood, from nest
and hollow: all were hushed, not out of fright,
nor due to any ruse. They were possessed

with listening. Then howl, cry, and roar
grew small within their hearts. And where before
there was barely a place for guests to enter,

a hideout harboring all the darkest urges,
whose entryway was made of shaky birches –
in their hearing, you raised up a temple.

I.2

Und fast ein Mädchen wars und ging hervor
aus diesem einigen Glück von Sang und Leier
und glänzte klar durch ihre Frühlingsschleier
und machte sich ein Bett in meinem Ohr.

Und schlief in mir. Und alles war ihr Schlaf.
Die Bäume, die ich je bewundert, diese
fühlbare Ferne, die gefühlte Wiese
und jedes Staunen, das mich selbst betraf.

Sie schlief die Welt. Singender Gott, wie hast
du sie vollendet, daß sie nicht begehrte,
erst wach zu sein? Sieh, sie erstand und schlief.

Wo ist ihr Tod? O, wirst du dies Motiv
erfinden noch, eh sich dein Lied verzehrte? –
Wo sinkt sie hin aus mir? . . . Ein Mädchen fast . . .

I.2

It was almost a girl who issued out
from this happy accord of song and lyre
and glowed translucent through her springtime shroud
and made herself a bed within my ear.

And slept in me. And everything was her sleep:
the trees that I looked up to, the unhidden
distances, the meadow I could feel,
and every wonder I myself was given.

She slept the world. Singing god, how then
did you fulfill her that she never hoped
to be awake? See, she got up and slept.

Where is her death? O, could you still compose
this theme before your song dissolves itself?
Where does she sink from me? . . . A girl, almost.

I.3

Ein Gott vermags. Wie aber, sag mir, soll
ein Mann ihm folgen durch die schmale Leier?
Sein Sinn ist Zwiespalt. An der Kreuzung zweier
Herzwege steht kein Tempel für Apoll.

Gesang, wie du ihn lehrst, ist nicht Begehr,
nicht Werbung um ein endlich noch Erreichtes;
Gesang ist Dasein. Für den Gott ein Leichtes.
Wann aber *sind* wir? Und wann wendet *er*

an unser Sein die Erde und die Sterne?
Dies *ists* nicht, Jüngling, daß du liebst, wenn auch
die Stimme dann den Mund dir aufstößt, – lerne

vergessen, daß du aufsangst. Das verrinnt.
In Wahrheit singen, ist ein andrer Hauch.
Ein Hauch um nichts. Ein Wehn im Gott. Ein Wind.

I.3

A god can do it. But how, tell me, does
a man follow him through the narrow harp?
His mind is divided. Where two cross at once
on heart-ways, there's no temple for Apollo.

Song, as you describe it, isn't longing,
not a plea for some end to be completed.
Song is existence – easy for a god,
but when do we exist? And when does *he*

turn the earth and stars around our being?
Not when you're young and in love, even if
your voice erupts in tongues at such a time.

Learn to forget that song – it will decline.
True singing needs another way to breathe.
A "nothing" breath. A gust of god. A wind.

I.4

O ihr Zärtlichen, tretet zuweilen
in den Atem, der euch nicht meint,
laßt ihn an eueren Wangen sich teilen,
hinter euch zittert er, wieder vereint.

O ihr Seligen, o ihr Heilen,
die ihr der Anfang der Herzen scheint.
Bogen der Pfeile und Ziele von Pfeilen,
ewiger glänzt euer Lächeln verweint.

Fürchtet euch nicht zu leiden, die Schwere,
gebt sie zurück an der Erde Gewicht;
schwer sind die Berge, schwer sind die Meere.

Selbst die als Kinder ihr pflanztet, die Bäume,
wurden zu schwer längst; ihr trüget sie nicht.
Aber die Lüfte . . . aber die Räume . . .

I.4

Oh you gentle ones, from time to time
step directly into a foreign breath;
as it passes your cheeks, let it divide:
behind it swirls, becoming one again.

You who are blissful, and you the undamaged,
who appear where all hearts have their source;
bows made of arrows and targets of arrows,
even through tears your smile constantly glows.

Don't recoil from suffering: the weight,
bring it back to the gravity of the earth.
Heavy are the mountains, heavy the seas.

When you were children, you gave root to trees
that grew unbearably weighty, even at first.
Still, the air . . . still, the open spaces . . .

I.5

Errichtet keinen Denkstein. Laßt die Rose
nur jedes Jahr zu seinen Gunsten blühn.
Denn Orpheus ists. Seine Metamorphose
in dem und dem. Wir sollen uns nicht mühn

um andre Namen. Ein für alle Male
ists Orpheus, wenn es singt. Er kommt und geht.
Ists nicht schon viel, wenn er die Rosenschale
um ein paar Tage manchmal übersteht?

O wie er schwinden muß, daß ihrs begrifft!
Und wenn ihm selbst auch bangte, daß er schwände.
Indem sein Wort das Hiersein übertrifft,

ist er schon dort, wohin ihrs nicht begleitet.
Der Leier Gitter zwängt ihm nicht die Hände.
Und er gehorcht, indem er überschreitet.

I.5

Erect no gravestone; only, let the rose
bloom every year in memory of him.
For this is Orpheus. His metamorph-
osis is here, in this and that. Admit,

then, of no other name. Once and for all:
where there is song, it's Orpheus. He comes
and goes. Isn't it something, for a small
while, if he outlives the flower buds?

He has to vanish so you'll understand!
Although he dreads that vanishing, and though
his every word exceeds this place and time,

he's there already – where you cannot go.
The instrument does not constrain his hands,
and as he steps beyond, he toes the line.

I.6

Ist er ein Hiesiger? Nein, aus beiden
Reichen erwuchs seine weite Natur.
Kundiger böge die Zweige der Weiden,
wer die Wurzeln der Weiden erfuhr.

Geht ihr zu Bette, so laßt auf dem Tische
Brot nicht und Milch nicht; die Toten ziehts –.
Aber er, der Beschwörende, mische
unter der Milde des Augenlids

ihre Erscheinung in alles Geschaute;
und der Zauber von Erdrauch und Raute
sei ihm so wahr wie der klarste Bezug.

Nichts kann das gültige Bild ihm verschlimmern;
sei es aus Gräbern, sei es aus Zimmern,
rühme er Fingerring, Spange und Krug.

I.6

Is he at home here? No, out of both
regions his extensive nature bloomed.
Able to bend the willow boughs are those
who have understood the willow's roots.

When you go to bed, leave out no milk
or bread on the table: this attracts the dead.
But he, the conjuror, invite him in
underneath the eyelids' gentle red

to mix appearance into all that's seen;
and let the magic of fumitory and rue
be as real to him as the clearest thing.

Nothing can tarnish this authentic scene;
whether it be from graves or living-rooms,
let him admire necklace, jug, and ring.

I.7

Rühmen, das ists! Ein zum Rühmen Bestellter,
ging er hervor wie das Erz aus des Steins
Schweigen. Sein Herz, o vergängliche Kelter
eines den Menschen unendlichen Weins.

Nie versagt ihm die Stimme am Staube,
wenn ihn das göttliche Beispiel ergreift.
Alles wird Weinberg, alles wird Traube,
in seinem fühlenden Süden gereift.

Nicht in den Grüften der Könige Moder
straft ihm die Rühmung lügen, oder
daß von den Göttern ein Schatten fällt.

Er ist einer der bleibenden Boten,
der noch weit in die Türen der Toten
Schalen mit rühmlichen Früchten hält.

I.7

Praising, that's it! He was meant to praise,
and flowed like ore out of the quiet stone.
His heart – it was an evanescent press
that made an ageless wine for us alone.

When he's within a sacred instant's grip,
his voice is never dusty or dried out.
Everything turns to vineyard, turns to grape,
mellowing in his tender, sentient south.

Neither the growth of mold in royal vaults,
nor any shadow cast down by the gods,
could ever undercut his songs of praise.

He is the patient herald who remains,
delivering the most praiseworthy bowls
of fruit to the dead, who lie beyond the door.

I.8

Nur im Raum der Rühmung darf die Klage
gehn, die Nymphe des geweinten Quells,
wachend über unserm Niederschlage,
daß er klar sei an demselben Fels,

der die Tore trägt und die Altäre. –
Sieh, um ihre stillen Schultern früht
das Gefühl, daß sie die jüngste wäre
unter den Geschwistern im Gemüt.

Jubel *weiß*, und Sehnsucht ist geständig, –
nur die Klage lernt noch; mädchenhändig
zählt sie nächtelang das alte Schlimme.

Aber plötzlich, schräg und ungeübt,
hält sie doch ein Sternbild unsrer Stimme
in den Himmel, den ihr Hauch nicht trübt.

I.8

Only in the realm of praising may Lament
drift, nymph of the teardrop-nourished brook,
who oversees our hearts' disheartenment,
making our crying strike the very rock

that raises up the altars and the gates.
Look – around her silent shoulders comes
the dawning knowledge that she came here late;
among the sisters, she is the most young.

Rejoicing *knows*, and Longing has confessed –
only Lament still learns; with gentle hands,
she reckons every night the ancient wrong.

But suddenly, impromptu and askance,
she holds a constellation of our song
against a sky untroubled by her breath.

I.9

Nur wer die Leier schon hob
auch unter Schatten,
darf das unendliche Lob
ahnend erstatten.

Nur wer mit Toten vom Mohn
aß, von dem ihren,
wird nicht den leisesten Ton
wieder verlieren.

Mag auch die Spieglung im Teich
oft uns verschwimmen:
Wisse das Bild.

Erst in dem Doppelbereich
werden die Stimmen
ewig und mild.

I.9

Someone who's already lifted
his lyre among shades
may regain a premonition
of endless praise.

Someone who's dined with the dead,
on poppies of their own,
will never again forget
the gentlest tone.

Although, to us, reflections often
dissolve on the water:
know the picture.

Only in another zone
do voices first grow
kind and persistent.

I.10

Euch, die ihr nie mein Gefühl verließt,
grüß ich, antikische Sarkophage,
die das fröhliche Wasser römischer Tage
als ein wandelndes Lied durchfließt.

Oder jene so offenen, wie das Aug
eines frohen erwachenden Hirten,
– innen voll Stille und Bienensaug –
denen entzückte Falter entschwirrten;

alle, die man dem Zweifel entreißt,
grüß ich, die wiedergeöffneten Munde,
die schon wußten, was schweigen heißt.

Wissen wirs, Freunde, wissen wirs nicht?
Beides bildet die zögernde Stunde
in dem menschlichen Angesicht.

I.10

You ancient tombs, who never have been lost
to me, I greet you, feeling warm at heart;
you, through whom the Roman water frolics
and every day goes wandering like a song.

Or those who are wide open as the eyes
of a contented shepherd on waking up
– full of quiet and of honeysuckle –
around which flit ecstatic butterflies.

I welcome all who wrest away from doubt,
and all who open up their mouths again,
already having sounded silence out.

Do we know what it means or not, my friends?
The hesitating hour shapes them both
into an echo of the human form.

I.11

Sieh den Himmel. Heißt kein Sternbild 'Reiter'?
Denn dies ist uns seltsam eingeprägt:
dieser Stolz aus Erde. Und ein Zweiter,
der ihn treibt und hält und den er trägt.

Ist nicht so, gejagt und dann gebändigt,
diese sehnige Natur des Seins?
Weg und Wendung. Doch ein Druck verständigt.
Neue Weite. Und die zwei sind eins.

Aber *sind* sie's? Oder meinen beide
nicht den Weg, den sie zusammen tun?
Namenlos schon trennt sie Tisch und Weide.

Auch die sternische Verbindung trügt.
Doch uns freue eine Weile nun
der Figur zu glauben. Das genügt.

I.11

Look at the sky. Is not one constellation
named "Rider"? For this earthly pride is all
too oddly marked in us. And there's a neighbor,
who drives and rides and brings it to a halt.

Isn't this being driven and restrained
just like the sinewy nature of our life?
Roadway and turn-off. But a touch explains.
New vast expanses. And the two unite.

But *are* they quite united? Don't they want
to take this path together? Even now,
from house to field both are kept from speaking.

Even celestial signs can be deceiving.
For just a little while, though, let's allow
ourselves to trust the image. This is enough.

I.12

Heil dem Geist, der uns verbinden mag;
denn wir leben wahrhaft in Figuren.
Und mit kleinen Schritten gehn die Uhren
neben unserm eigentlichen Tag.

Ohne unsern wahren Platz zu kennen,
handeln wir aus wirklichem Bezug.
Die Antennen fühlen die Antennen,
und die leere Ferne trug . . .

Reine Spannung. O Musik der Kräfte!
Ist nicht durch die läßlichen Geschäfte
jede Störung von dir abgelenkt?

Selbst wenn sich der Bauer sorgt und handelt,
wo die Saat in Sommer sich verwandelt,
reicht er niemals hin. Die Erde *schenkt*.

I.12

Praise to the spirit who can find a way
of binding us, because we live in figures.
Clocks march with measured paces, and the minutes
tick off alongside our momentous day.

Of where we really are we're unaware,
and yet we act as though it all pertains.
Antennas feel for other antennas, with
a sense across the empty distances. . . .

Electric tension. Music of pure force!
Doesn't our petty business interfere
with your remote transmission on the air?

For all his worried labor and concern,
the farmer never digs to where seeds turn
deep soil into summer. Earth *bestows*.

I.13

Voller Apfel, Birne und Banane,
Stachelbeere . . . Alles dieses spricht
Tod und Leben in den Mund . . . Ich ahne . . .
Lest es einem Kind vom Angesicht,

wenn es sie erschmeckt. Dies kommt von weit.
Wird euch langsam namenlos im Munde?
Wo sonst Worte waren, fließen Funde,
aus dem Fruchtfleisch überrascht befreit.

Wagt zu sagen, was ihr Apfel nennt.
Diese Süße, die sich erst verdichtet,
um, im Schmecken leise aufgerichtet,

klar zu werden, wach und transparent,
doppeldeutig, sonnig, erdig, hiesig – :
O Erfahrung, Fühlung, Freude –, riesig!

I.13

Full ripe apple, banana and pear,
gooseberry. . . . All of these speak
of death and life in the mouth, I feel. . . .
Gather this from a child's face,

devouring. It comes from far away.
What's growing slowly nameless in your mouth?
In place of words, new drifts are found,
released from the fruit's pulp, amazed.

Just try to say what "apple" means.
This concentrated sweetness is growing
transparent, lucid, wide-awake,

emerging with a salient taste.
Two-sided, sunny, earthy, here –
experience, feeling, joy – enormous!

I.14

Wir gehen um mit Blume, Weinblatt, Frucht.
Sie sprechen nicht die Sprache nur des Jahres.
Aus Dunkel steigt ein buntes Offenbares
und hat vielleicht den Glanz der Eifersucht

der Toten an sich, die die Erde stärken.
Was wissen wir von ihrem Teil an dem?
Es ist seit lange ihre Art, den Lehm
mit ihrem freien Marke zu durchmärken.

Nun fragt sich nur: tun sie es gern? . . .
Drängt diese Frucht, ein Werk von schweren Sklaven,
geballt zu uns empor, zu ihren Herrn?

Sind *sie* die Herrn, die bei den Wurzeln schlafen,
und gönnen uns aus ihren Überflüssen
dies Zwischending aus stummer Kraft und Küssen?

I.14

We are involved in flower, vine, and fruit:
they speak not only the language of the year.
Out of the dark appears a leafy shoot,
its green suggestive of the jealous leer

of those now dead who fructify the earth.
About their part in this, what can we know?
For so long they have brought about the birth
of clay, with the stray marrow of their bones.

So here's the question: is it gladly done? . . .
Or is this fruit a clenched fist raised by slaves,
worn down by toil, toward us, the ones above?

Or could *they* be in charge, asleep in graves
beside the roots, and giving from their surfeit
this hybrid of mute vigor and of kisses?

I.15

Wartet . . . , das schmeckt . . . Schon ists auf der Flucht.
. . . Wenig Musik nur, ein Stampfen, ein Summen – :
Mädchen, ihr warmen, Mädchen, ihr stummen,
tanzt den Geschmack der erfahrenen Frucht!

Tanzt die Orange. Wer kann sie vergessen,
wie sie, ertrinkend in sich, sich wehrt
wider ihr Süßsein. Ihr habt sie besessen.
Sie hat sich köstlich zu euch bekehrt.

Tanzt die Orange. Die wärmere Landschaft,
werft sie aus euch, daß die reife erstrahle
in Lüften der Heimat! Erglühte, enthüllt

Düfte um Düfte. Schafft die Verwandtschaft
mit der reinen, sich weigernden Schale,
mit dem Saft, der die Glückliche füllt!

I.15

Wait . . . this flavor . . . it's already fading.
A piece of music, stamping feet, a hum –
young women, with your silences inflamed,
now dance for what you know is on your tongue!

Dance the orange. Who cannot remember
the way it labors, drowning in its own
sweetness? So delectable and tender,
after this conversion it is yours.

Dance the orange. Throw its warmer landscape
away from you, until the ripeness shines
amid these native breezes! Peel away

each aroma, making new relations
with the pure, the self-restraining rind,
and with the flavorable juice inside!

I.16

Du, mein Freund, bist einsam, weil . . .
Wir machen mit Worten und Fingerzeigen
uns allmählich die Welt zu eigen,
vielleicht ihren schwächsten, gefährlichsten Teil.

Wer zeigt mit Fingern auf einen Geruch? –
Doch von den Kräften, die uns bedrohten,
fühlst du viele . . . Du kennst die Toten,
und du erschrickst vor dem Zauberspruch.

Sieh, nun heißt es zusammen ertragen
Stückwerk und Teile, als sei es das Ganze.
Dir helfen, wird schwer sein. Vor allem: pflanze

mich nicht in dein Herz. Ich wüchse zu schnell.
Doch *meines* Herrn Hand will ich führen und sagen:
Hier. Das ist Esau in seinem Fell.

I.16

Creaturely friend, you are so alone
because . . . with words and fingertips
we gradually make the world our own,
including its most delicate bits.

Who points a finger toward a scent?
Out of the powers that cause us alarm,
you feel many . . . you know the dead
and cower before the sorcerer's charm.

See, both of us must always bear
patches and scraps, as if complete.
To help you is hard. Don't plant me in

your heart, for I would grow too deep.
But I'll guide *my* master's hand and say:
here, this is Esau in his skin.

I.17

Zu unterst der Alte, verworrn,
all der Erbauten
Wurzel, verborgener Born,
den sie nie schauten.

Sturmhelm und Jägerhorn,
Spruch von Ergrauten,
Männer im Bruderzorn,
Frauen wie Lauten . . .

Drängender Zweig an Zweig,
nirgends ein freier . . .
Einer! O steig . . . o steig . . .

Aber sie brechen noch.
Dieser erst oben doch
biegt sich zur Leier.

I.17

Under all well-founded things,
an entangled root there lies
hidden, like the secret spring
from which all of them arise.

War helmet, horn of the gunners,
age-weary truths,
wrath among brothers,
and women like lutes . . .

The branches cramp each other,
none of them free –
but one! Climb – go higher . . .

Still, they break one another.
At the top of the tree,
one bends into a lyre.

I.18

Hörst du das Neue, Herr,
dröhnen und beben?
Kommen Verkündiger,
die es erheben.

Zwar ist kein Hören heil
in dem Durchtobtsein,
doch der Maschinenteil
will jetzt gelobt sein.

Sieh, die Maschine:
wie sie sich wälzt und rächt
und uns entstellt und schwächt.

Hat sie aus uns auch Kraft,
sie, ohne Leidenschaft,
treibe und diene.

I.18

Do you hear the New, mister,
rumble and quake?
Here come the announcers
to herald its name.

There is no safe hearing
amidst the uproar,
but all this machinery
needs our support.

See the Machine:
it turns and gets revenge,
leaving us impaired.

Yet we give it strength,
so let it be restrained
to propel and serve.

I.19

Wandelt sich rasch auch die Welt
wie Wolkengestalten,
alles Vollendete fällt
heim zum Uralten.

Über dem Wandel und Gang,
weiter und freier,
währt noch dein Vor-Gesang,
Gott mit der Leier.

Nicht sind die Leiden erkannt,
nicht ist die Liebe gelernt,
und was im Tod uns entfernt,

ist nicht entschleiert.
Einzig das Lied überm Land
heiligt und feiert.

I.19

Despite the ferment of the world,
changing like the shapes of clouds,
all completed things return
home to their primordial ground.

Above change and wandering,
more free and higher,
your overture still endures,
god of the lyre.

Suffering hasn't been fathomed,
nor love understood,
and that which death erases

remains no less obscure.
Song alone over the land
keeps holy and praises.

I.20

Dir aber, Herr, o was weih ich dir, sag,
der das Ohr den Geschöpfen gelehrt? –
Mein Erinnern an einen Frühlingstag,
seinen Abend, in Rußland –, ein Pferd . . .

Herüber vom Dorf kam der Schimmel allein,
an der vorderen Fessel den Pflock,
um die Nacht auf den Wiesen allein zu sein;
wie schlug seiner Mähne Gelock

an den Hals im Takte des Übermuts,
bei dem grob gehemmten Galopp.
Wie sprangen die Quellen des Rossebluts!

Der fühlte die Weiten, und ob!
Der sang und der hörte –, dein Sagenkreis
war *in* ihm geschlossen.
            Sein Bild: ich weih's.

I.20

You, who make all creatures able to hear,
oh poet, tell me: what can I dedicate
to you? I remember one spring day,
near dusk, in Russia, when a horse appeared.

Across the village he came up alone,
all white, a hobble fettering one leg,
to camp out in the pasture on his own;
how that curled mane beat against his neck,

keeping time with his animated spirit –
despite the awkwardly impeded gallop.
And how his stallion-blood rushed from the source!

He felt the open distances. He sang
and listened – and your cycle of songs became
complete in him. This image: it is yours.

I.21

Frühling ist wiedergekommen. Die Erde
ist wie ein Kind, das Gedichte weiß;
viele, o viele . . . Für die Beschwerde
langen Lernens bekommt sie den Preis.

Streng war ihr Lehrer. Wir mochten das Weiße
an dem Barte des alten Manns.
Nun, wie das Grüne, das Blaue heiße,
dürfen wir fragen: sie kanns, sie kanns!

Erde, die frei hat, du glückliche, spiele
nun mit den Kindern. Wir wollen dich fangen,
fröhliche Erde. Dem Frohsten gelingts.

O, was der Lehrer sie lehrte, das Viele,
und was gedruckt steht in Wurzeln und langen
schwierigen Stämmen: sie singts, sie singts!

I.21

Spring is arriving back again. The earth
is like a child reciting many poems
she's memorized by heart. Her prize is worth
the effort spent on what is now disclosed.

Her teacher was severe. We loved the white
hair all throughout the old man's hoary beard.
Now we can ask her what green colors might
mean, or blue: and she knows every word!

Fortunate earth, enjoy your holiday –
play with the kids, and watch us try in vain
to catch you. Only the happiest survives.

Oh, her teacher has shown so many things:
all that's written in roots, and all the signs
inscribed on intricate twigs. And now she sings!

I.22

Wir sind die Treibenden.
Aber den Schritt der Zeit,
nehmt ihn als Kleinigkeit
im immer Bleibenden.

Alles das Eilende
wird schon vorüber sein;
denn das Verweilende
erst weiht uns ein.

Knaben, o werft den Mut
nicht in die Schnelligkeit,
nicht in den Flugversuch.

Alles ist ausgeruht:
Dunkel und Helligkeit,
Blume und Buch.

I.22

What's driving is us;
yet the pace of time
is nothing but dust
next to what abides.

For everything hurried,
it's already night.
Only the enduring
can sanction our life.

O children, don't waste
your bravery in racing
around or being flighty.

All things now stay put:
darkness and brightness,
both flower and book.

I.23

O erst *dann*, wenn der Flug
nicht mehr um seinetwillen
wird in die Himmelstillen
steigen, sich selber genug,

um in lichten Profilen,
als das Gerät, das gelang,
Liebling der Winde zu spielen,
sicher, schwenkend und schlank, –

erst, wenn ein reines Wohin
wachsender Apparate
Knabenstolz überwiegt,

wird, überstürzt von Gewinn,
jener den Fernen Genahte
sein, was er einsam erfliegt.

I.23

Only *then*, when flight
no more for its own sake
ascends into the still sky,
sufficient, self-contained,

so that it gleams again,
with contours well-designed,
to play the lover of the wind,
secure, lean, and alive –

not until a pure frontier
outweighs puerile complacency
about the latest contrivance

will someone, flushed with victory
and bringing distant places near,
be what he is alone in flying.

I.24

Sollen wir unsere uralte Freundschaft, die großen
niemals werbenden Götter, weil sie der harte
Stahl, den wir streng erzogen, nicht kennt, verstoßen
oder sie plötzlich suchen auf einer Karte?

Diese gewaltigen Freunde, die uns die Toten
nehmen, rühren nirgends an unsere Räder.
Unsere Gastmähler haben wir weit –, unsere Bäder,
fortgerückt, und ihre uns lang schon zu langsamen Boten

überholen wir immer. Einsamer nun auf einander
ganz angewiesen, ohne einander zu kennen,
führen wir nicht mehr die Pfade als schöne Mäander,

sondern als Grade. Nur noch in Dampfkesseln brennen
die einstigen Feuer und heben die Hämmer, die immer
größern. Wir aber nehmen an Kraft ab, wie Schwimmer.

I.24

Shall we disown our oldest friendships, those
vast undemanding deities, since that
hard metal we have tempered never chose
to know them? Or try to find them on a map?

All of these potent friends, who take the dead
from us – they never even touch our wheels.
We've moved too far away: our baths and feasts
take place beyond their messengers. Ahead,

we leave them in the dust. Now, more alone,
not knowing one another, we depend
on what we do not know. Our roads are straight,

and don't meander back upon themselves.
The pistons lift in boilers where the old
flame burns. Yet, as we swim, our powers fail.

I.25

Dich aber will ich nun, *Dich*, die ich kannte
wie eine Blume, von der ich den Namen nicht weiß,
noch *ein* Mal erinnern und ihnen zeigen, Entwandte,
schöne Gespielin des unüberwindlichen Schrei's.

Tänzerin erst, die plötzlich, den Körper voll Zögern,
anhielt, als göß man ihr Jungsein in Erz;
trauernd und lauschend –. Da, von den hohen Vermögern
fiel ihr Musik in das veränderte Herz.

Nah war die Krankheit. Schon von den Schatten bemächtigt,
drängte verdunkelt das Blut, doch, wie flüchtig verdächtigt,
trieb es in seinen natürlichen Frühling hervor.

Wieder und wieder, von Dunkel und Sturz unterbrochen,
glänzte es irdisch. Bis es nach schrecklichem Pochen
trat in das trostlos offene Tor.

I.25

But *you*, whom I knew like a flower whose name
I didn't know, you were somehow bound to die,
and *now* I will recall you, show you to them,
gorgeous playfellow of the unthwarted cry.

Dancer at first, whose body hesitated,
then stopped – as if her youth were cast in bronze.
Lamentation, listening. Then, from the great
makers, music fell into her altered heart.

Sickness was near. Already mastered by shadows,
her darkened blood, suspicious, couldn't wait;
it surged forth toward its natural springtime.

Again and again, through darkness and disaster,
it glowed, earthly. Only horrible beating
sent it through the hopelessly open gate.

I.26

Du aber, Göttlicher, du, bis zuletzt noch Ertöner,
da ihn der Schwarm der verschmähten Mänaden befiel,
hast ihr Geschrei übertönt mit Ordnung, du Schöner,
aus den Zerstörenden stieg dein erbauendes Spiel.

Keine war da, daßss sie Haupt dir und Leier zerstör.
Wwie sie auch rangen und rasten, und alle die scharfen
Steine, die sie nach deinem Herzen warfen,
wurden zu Sanftem an dir und begabt mit Gehör.

Schließlich zerschlugen sie dich, von der Rache gehetzt,
während dein Klang noch in Löwen und Felsen verweilte
und in den Bäumen und Vögeln. Dort singst du noch jetzt.

O du verlorener Gott! Du unendliche Spur!
Nur weil dich reißend zuletzt die Feindschaft verteilte,
sind wir die Hörenden jetzt und ein Mund der Natur.

I.26

And you, divine one, sounding until the end,
even when besieged by a swarm of maenads –
you beautifully drowned out their violent yell,
a voice of order prevailing over the chaos.

None of them could destroy your head or harp,
however much they struggled. All of the sharp
stones thrown in rage at you turned soft upon
approaching, suddenly able to hear your song.

At last they killed you, in retaliation,
but in the aftermath your music rings –
in rocks and trees, lions and birds, you sing.

Oh, vanished god! Your everlasting mark!
Since their hatred has torn you apart,
we alone are the ears and mouth of nature.

II.1

Atmen, du unsichtbares Gedicht!
Immerfort um das eigne
Sein rein eingetauschter Weltraum. Gegengewicht,
in dem ich mich rhythmisch ereigne.

Einzige Welle, deren
allmähliches Meer ich bin;
sparsamstes du von allen möglichen Meeren, –
Raumgewinn.

Wieviele von diesen Stellen der Räume waren schon
innen in mir. Manche Winde
sind wie mein Sohn.

Erkennst du mich, Luft, du, voll noch einst meiniger Orte?
Du, einmal glatte Rinde,
Rundung und Blatt meiner Worte.

II.1

Breathing, you unseeable poem!
Constantly in exchange between
our existence and the space of the world.
Counterweight where I rhythmically come to be.

Solitary wave, in which
I am the gradual sea.
Most sparing of all possible waters,
you win space eventually.

How many places have already been
inhaled by me – many a wind
is like my own child.

Do you know me, air, full of my traces?
You were once the trunk, rind,
and greenery of my phrases.

II.2

So wie dem Meister manchmal das eilig
nähere Blatt den *wirklichen* Strich
abnimmt: so nehmen oft Spiegel das heilig
einzige Lächeln der Mädchen in sich,

wenn sie den Morgen erproben, allein, –
oder im Glanze der dienenden Lichter.
Und in das Atmen der echten Gesichter,
später, fällt nur ein Widerschein.

Was haben Augen einst ins umrußte
lange Verglühn der Kamine geschaut:
Blicke des Lebens, für immer verlorne.

Ach, der Erde, wer kennt die Verluste?
Nur, wer mit dennoch preisendem Laut
sänge das Herz, das ins Ganze geborne.

II.2

Sometimes a scrap of paper close at hand
is canvas for the master's *genuine* work;
so mirrors often capture in a glance
the sacred and distinctive smiles of girls

as they survey the morning, all alone –
or, in the hidden glow of indoor lights.
What real and breathing faces later show
is just a dim reflection or disguise.

These eyes that look into the blackening coals
of a slow-dying fire: what have they seen?
Glimpses of life, forever exhausted.

Earth, who comprehends your losses?
Only the one who nonetheless can sing
in praise, with heart delivered into the whole.

II.3

Spiegel: noch nie hat man wissend beschrieben,
was ihr in euerem Wesen seid.
Ihr, wie mit lauter Löchern von Sieben
erfüllten Zwischenräume der Zeit.

Ihr, noch des leeren Saales Verschwender –,
wenn es dämmert, wie Wälder weit . . .
Und der Lüster geht wie ein Sechzehn-Ender
durch eure Unbetretbarkeit.

Manchmal seid ihr voll Malerei.
Einige scheinen *in* euch gegangen –,
andere schicktet ihr scheu vorbei.

Aber die Schönste wird bleiben –, bis
drüben in ihre enthaltenen Wangen
eindrang der klare gelöste Narziß.

II.3

Mirrors: no one has ever yet described
your essence, for we don't know what it is.
You fill the intervening space of time
as openly as holes throughout a sieve.

You are the wastrels in the vacant hall –
when twilight arrives, wide as a grove of trees.
And, like a trophy stag, the luster vaults
across your inaccessible boundary.

Often you are filled with pictures. Some
appear to have already entered you,
while others you have gently sent away.

But she remains, the most beautiful one,
until Narcissus finally breaks through
and makes his way to her concealed face.

II.4

O dieses ist das Tier, das es nicht giebt.
Sie wußtens nicht und habens jeden Falls
– sein Wandeln, seine Haltung, seinen Hals,
bis in des stillen Blickes Licht – geliebt.

Zwar *war* es nicht. Doch weil sie's liebten, ward
ein reines Tier. Sie ließen immer Raum.
Und in dem Raume, klar und ausgespart,
erhob es leicht sein Haupt und brauchte kaum

zu sein. Sie nährten es mit keinem Korn,
nur immer mit der Möglichkeit, es sei.
Und die gab solche Stärke an das Tier,

daß es aus sich ein Stirnhorn trieb. Ein Horn.
Zu einer Jungfrau kam es weiß herbei –
und war im Silber-Spiegel und in ihr.

II.4

This is the animal that does not exist.
They didn't know this, and – in any case,
they loved it – neck and footsteps, even its
demeanor and the light of its mild gaze.

It never *did* exist. But from their love
this pure being came to be. They gave it room,
and in that clear space, desolate enough,
it raised its head up out of the cocoon

of nonexistence. So they fed it, not
with grain, but with the possibility
of being. And the creature grew so strong,

out of its brow a single horn emerged.
All white, it showed up for a girl, and she
perceived it – in the mirror, and in her.

II.5

Blumenmuskel, der der Anemone
Wiesenmorgen nach und nach erschließt,
bis in ihren Schoß das polyphone
Licht der lauten Himmel sich ergießt,

in den stillen Blütenstern gespannter
Muskel des unendlichen Empfangs,
manchmal *so* von Fülle übermannter,
daß der Ruhewink des Untergangs

kaum vermag die weitzurückgeschnellten
Blätterränder dir zurückzugeben:
du, Entschluß und Kraft von *wie*viel Welten!

Wir Gewaltsamen, wir währen länger.
Aber *wann*, in welchem aller Leben,
sind wir endlich offen und Empfänger?

II.5

Flower-flesh, unfolding bit by bit
this anemone in the meadow dawn,
until its loins are open to the light
of many sounds the loud sky gushes down;

muscle of infinite receptivity,
you flex within the silent flower-star,
at times *so* overwhelmed by superfluity
that the gentle beckoning and calm

of sunset can just barely realign
all these hyperextended petal edges:
determination of *how many* worlds!

We violent ones, we finally endure.
But when – that is, in which of all our lives,
can we at last be open and receptive?

II.6

Rose, du thronende, denen im Altertume
warst du ein Kelch mit einfachem Rand.
Uns aber bist du die volle zahllose Blume,
der unerschöpfliche Gegenstand.

In deinem Reichtum scheinst du wie Kleidung um Kleidung
um einen Leib aus nichts als Glanz;
aber dein einzelnes Blatt ist zugleich die Vermeidung
und die Verleugnung jedes Gewands.

Seit Jahrhunderten ruft uns dein Duft
seine süßesten Namen herüber;
plötzlich liegt er wie Ruhm in der Luft.

Dennoch, wir wissen ihn nicht zu nennen, wir raten . . .
Und Erinnerung geht zu ihm über,
die wir von rufbaren Stunden erbaten.

II.6

Rose, enthroned one, you in ancient times
were just a flower with a simple cup.
Now you are the inexhaustible blossom,
blooming on innumerably for us.

In your finery, you seem to be
layers of clothes around a body made
of light; yet every petal is at once
an undraped body nakedly displayed.

For centuries your scent has beckoned us,
as if it whispered sweet familiar things;
then, suddenly, it fills the air like fame.

We guess your name, and yet we cannot know.
Our memory is invaded by a fragrance,
summoning what we held in mind before.

II.7

Blumen, ihr schließlich den ordnenden Händen verwandte,
(Händen der Mädchen von einst und jetzt),
die auf dem Gartentisch oft von Kante zu Kante
lagen, ermattet und sanft verletzt,

wartend des Wassers, das sie noch einmal erhole
aus dem begonnenen Tod –, und nun
wieder erhobene zwischen die strömenden Pole
fühlender Finger, die wohlzutun

mehr noch vermögen, als ihr ahntet, ihr leichten,
wenn ihr euch wiederfandet im Krug,
langsam erkühlend und Warmes der Mädchen, wie Beichten,

von euch gebend, wie trübe ermüdende Sünden,
die das Gepflücktsein beging, als Bezug
wieder zu ihnen, die sich euch blühend verbünden.

II.7

Flowers, related at last to arranging hands
(feminine hands, in the past and even still),
you often lay across the garden table,
slightly injured and beginning to wilt,

waiting for the rain that might revive you
just a while, since death is setting in –
and now you're lifted up between the beams
of sympathetic fingers once again,

whose gentle touch is able to support
your waking in the vase. Then, as you cool
slowly, breathing out the warmth of girls,

draining like the taint of sins confessed,
committed with your picking, you renew
a bond of kinship with your friends in bloom.

II.8

Wenige ihr, der einstigen Kindheit Gespielen
in den zerstreuten Gärten der Stadt:
wie wir uns fanden und uns zögernd gefielen
und, wie das Lamm mit dem redenden Blatt,

sprachen als Schweigende. Wenn wir uns einmal freuten,
keinem gehörte es. Wessen wars?
Und wie zergings unter allen den gehenden Leuten
und im Bangen des langen Jahrs.

Wagen umrollten uns fremd, vorübergezogen,
Häuser umstanden uns stark, aber unwahr, – und keines
kannte uns je. *Was* war wirklich im All?

Nichts. Nur die Bälle. Ihre herrlichen Bogen.
Auch nicht die Kinder . . . Aber manchmal trat eines,
ach ein vergehendes, unter den fallenden Ball.

II.8

You few, my childhood playmates from a time
now lost, dispersed in all the city gardens:
we found and, cautiously, began to like
each other. As the lamb gives voice to darkness,

we spoke in silence. Then, when there was joy,
nobody owned it; whose joy could it be?
We saw it dissolve beneath the people's noise
and in the lengthy year's anxiety.

Unfamiliar vehicles wheeled past,
and houses stood around us, strong but false –
none knew us. What was real under the sun?

Nothing. Only the balls. Their marvelous paths.
Not even the children. . . . But sometimes one
would step, ephemeral, under a plummeting ball.

II.9

Rühmt euch, ihr Richtenden, nicht der entbehrlichen Folter
und daß das Eisen nicht länger an Hälsen sperrt.
Keins ist gesteigert, kein Herz –, weil ein gewollter
Krampf der Milde euch zarter verzerrt.

Was es durch Zeiten bekam, das schenkt das Schafott
wieder zurück, wie Kinder ihr Spielzeug vom vorig
alten Geburtstag. Ins reine, ins hohe, ins torig
offene Herz träte er anders, der Gott

wirklicher Milde. Er käme gewaltig und griffe
strahlender um sich, wie Göttliche sind.
Mehr als ein Wind für die großen gesicherten Schiffe.

Weniger nicht, als die heimliche leise Gewahrung,
die uns im Innern schweigend gewinnt
wie ein still spielendes Kind aus unendlicher Paarung.

II.9

You who judge, don't boast about omitting
torture – even if irons are inconvenient.
No one's heart is comforted, because
reluctant pangs of mercy made you lenient.

The scaffold will return what it's been given
for ages, just as children often trade
their birthday gifts. The real god of mercy
would find another manner to invade

the pure and open heart. He'd come to grip
it firmly, bathed in godlike radiant light.
More than a wind for large, complacent ships.

Nothing less than a silent understanding
that wins us over inwardly, at play
much like the child of some vast partnership.

II.10

Alles Erworbne bedroht die Maschine, solange
sie sich erdreistet, im Geist, statt im Gehorchen, zu sein.
Daß nicht der herrlichen Hand schöneres Zögern mehr prange,
zu dem entschlossenern Bau schneidet sie steifer den Stein.

Nirgends bleibt sie zurück, daß wir ihr *ein* Mal entrönnen
und sie in stiller Fabrik ölend sich selber gehört.
Sie ist das Leben, – sie meint es am besten zu können,
die mit dem gleichen Entschluß ordnet und schafft und zerstört.

Aber noch ist uns das Dasein verzaubert; an hundert
Stellen ist es noch Ursprung. Ein Spielen von reinen
Kräften, die keiner berührt, der nicht kniet und bewundert.

Worte gehen noch zart am Unsäglichen aus . . .
Und die Musik, immer neu, aus den bebendsten Steinen,
baut im unbrauchbaren Raum ihr vergöttlichtes Haus.

II.10

All that we have gained, the machine threatens –
once a tool assumes a force of its own.
Instead of letting us get used to mastery,
for buildings more severe it cuts the stone.

Nowhere does it pause and allow us to flee,
maintaining itself and leaving factories hushed.
It thinks itself alive – and with the same
state of mind it makes, arrays, destructs.

But life for us is still enchanted, in
a hundred places new. Pure force at play,
which strikes whoever sees it with amazement.

Words continue to fail before the nameless. . . .
And music, always new in vacant space,
builds a cobbled house where gods can live.

II.11

Manche, des Todes, entstand ruhig geordnete Regel,
weiterbezwingender Mensch, seit du im Jagen beharrst;
mehr doch als Falle und Netz, weiß ich dich, Streifen von Segel,
den man hinuntergehängt in den höhligen Karst.

Leise ließ man dich ein, als wärst du ein Zeichen,
Frieden zu feiern. Doch dann: rang dich am Rande der Knecht,
und, aus den Höhlen, die Nacht warf eine Handvoll von bleichen
taumelnden Tauben ins Licht . . .
Aber auch *das* ist im Recht.

Fern von dem Schauenden sei jeglicher Hauch des Bedauerns,
nicht nur vom Jäger allein, der, was sich zeitig erweist,
wachsam und handelnd vollzieht.

Töten ist eine Gestalt unseres wandernden Trauerns . . .
Rein ist im heiteren Geist,
was an uns selber geschieht.

II.11

Many a peacefully-rendered rule of death
came from the hunting of these desperados;
strip of cloth, I know you better than net
or trap. They hung you down in the Carso grottos.

They lowered you gently, gesturing (as it were)
in peace. But then their helper gave a tug,
and from those caves night flung a handful of birds,
dazed by the glare . . .
And *this* is somehow just.

Let any breath of regret be far from these
who oversee, not only the vigilant hunter,
who handily executes when the time arrives.

Killing is one form of our homeless grief . . .
Whatever may happen to us
turns pure in the radiant mind.

II.12

Wolle die Wandlung. O sei für die Flamme begeistert,
drin sich ein Ding dir entzieht, das mit Verwandlungen prunkt;
jener entwerfende Geist, welcher das Irdische meistert,
liebt in dem Schwung der Figur nichts wie den wendenden Punkt.

Was sich ins Bleiben verschließt, schon *ists* das Erstarrte;
wähnt es sich sicher im Schutz des unscheinbaren Grau's?
Warte, ein Härtestes warnt aus der Ferne das Harte.
Wehe – : abwesender Hammer holt aus!

Wer sich als Quelle ergießt, den erkennt die Erkennung;
und sie führt ihn entzückt durch das heiter Geschaffne,
das mit Anfang oft schließt und mit Ende beginnt.

Jeder glückliche Raum ist Kind oder Enkel von Trennung,
den sie staunend durchgehn. Und die verwandelte Daphne
will, seit sie lorbeern fühlt, daß du dich wandelst in Wind.

II.12

Seek transformation, yearning for the flame
in which proud alterations must be burned;
the spirit who charts out Earth's blueprint craves
above all points the one where something turns.

What sticks to mere survival soon gets rigid:
how safe is it to hide in a gray backyard?
Look – far away, an absent hammer is lifted.
The hardest sends forewarning to the hard.

Whoever overflows is known by Knowing;
she leads him, transfixed, through the fair creation
that often ends at the start and begins at the end.

Each happy space they walk through in amazement
is Exit's child or grandchild. And the transformed,
laurel Daphne wants you to turn to wind.

II.13

Sei allem Abschied voran, als wäre er hinter
dir, wie der Winter, der eben geht.
Denn unter Wintern ist einer so endlos Winter,
daß, überwinternd, dein Herz überhaupt übersteht.

Sei immer tot in Eurydike –, singender steige,
preisender steige zurück in den reinen Bezug.
Hier, unter Schwindenden, sei, im Reiche der Neige,
sei ein klingendes Glas, das sich im Klang schon zerschlug.

Sei – und wisse zugleich des Nicht-Seins Bedingung,
den unendlichen Grund deiner innigen Schwingung,
daß du sie völlig vollziehst dieses einzige Mal.

Zu dem gebrauchten sowohl, wie zum dumpfen und stummen
Vorrat der vollen Natur, den unsäglichen Summen,
zähle dich jubelnd hinzu und vernichte die Zahl.

II.13

Be ahead of all parting, just as if
it lay behind you like a passing season.
Among the winters, one (*so* endless) winter
will leave your over-wintered heart unbeaten.

Be forever dead in your love – but sing,
rise back up, and affirm the pure engagement.
Amid these fading and decaying things,
be the glass that rings out as it's breaking.

Be – but know the terms and limitations
of not-being, ground of your intimate vibration,
so that you fully meet them, even once.

Jubilantly with all that is dumb or deadened,
the unspeakable whole of nature's plenty,
number yourself as well – and annul the sum.

II.14

Siehe die Blumen, diese dem Irdischen treuen,
denen wir Schicksal vom Rande des Schicksals leihn, –
aber wer weiß es! Wenn sie ihr Welken bereuen,
ist es an uns, ihre Reue zu sein.

Alles will schweben. Da gehn wir umher wie Beschwerer,
legen auf alles uns selbst, vom Gewichte entzückt;
o was sind wir den Dingen für zehrende Lehrer,
weil ihnen ewige Kindheit glückt.

Nähme sie einer ins innige Schlafen und schliefe
tief mit den Dingen – : o wie käme er leicht,
anders zum anderen Tag, aus der gemeinsamen Tiefe.

Oder er bliebe vielleicht; und sie blühten und priesen
ihn, den Bekehrten, der nun den Ihrigen gleicht,
allen den stillen Geschwistern im Winde der Wiesen.

II.14

Perceive these flowers, faithful to the earth,
to which we lend a destiny from the edge
of fate – but who knows? If they face decay,
it's up to us to feel their regret.

All things arise. We trudge, as if weighed down,
pressing on everything, entranced with gravity.
What dreary teachers! Badly out of tune
with all that dwells in childhood everlasting.

And yet if someone brought them into sleep
completely, slept with things – how he'd awake
into a different day, from that same deep.

Or maybe he would stay; and they would thrive,
admitting him, a convert, to live among
his siblings in the field where calm air sweeps.

II.15

O Brunnen-Mund, du gebender, du Mund,
der unerschöpflich Eines, Reines, spricht, –
du, vor des Wassers fließendem Gesicht,
marmorne Maske. Und im Hintergrund

der Aquädukte Herkunft. Weither an
Gräbern vorbei, vom Hang des Apennins
tragen sie dir dein Sagen zu, das dann
am schwarzen Altern deines Kinns

vorüberfällt in das Gefäß davor.
Dies ist das schlafend hingelegte Ohr,
das Marmorohr, in das du immer sprichst.

Ein Ohr der Erde. Nur mit sich allein
redet sie also. Schiebt ein Krug sich ein,
so scheint es ihr, daß du sie unterbrichst.

II.15

O fountain-mouth, you never-ending giver,
with lips that always speak of one clear thing –
you marble mask faced up against the stream
of water. And way off there in the distance,

the origin of aqueducts. Out where
those gravestones lie, behind the Apennines,
they carry back to you your liquid sayings,
which flow down past your old, dark chin to find

themselves cascading into the basin there.
This is the ear laid on its side in slumber,
the marble ear to which your voice is given.

An ear of Earth. Although she's by herself,
she's always talking: dip a pitcher in,
and it will seem as if you interrupt her.

II.16

Immer wieder von uns aufgerissen,
ist der Gott die Stelle, welche heilt.
Wir sind Scharfe, denn wir wollen wissen,
aber er ist heiter und verteilt.

Selbst die reine, die geweihte Spende
nimmt er anders nicht in seine Welt,
als indem er sich dem freien Ende
unbewegt entgegenstellt.

Nur der Tote trinkt
aus der hier von uns *gehörten* Quelle,
wenn der Gott ihm schweigend winkt, dem Toten.

Uns wird nur das Lärmen angeboten.
Und das Lamm erbittet seine Schelle
aus dem stilleren Instinkt.

II.16

Always torn apart by us again,
Orpheus is still the place of healing.
We're all sharp-edged, because we want to know,
but he (the god) is everywhere serene.

Even the pure, the sacred offering,
is taken into his world no other way
except as he himself stands opposite
the open ending, motionless and staid.

Those alone who are dead are drinking
from this spring that's *heard* by us,
when the god provides a secret hint.

To *us*, only the noise is given.
And the lamb asks for the bell it wants
by virtue of a more quiet instinct.

II.17

Wo, in welchen immer selig bewässerten Gärten, an welchen
Bäumen, aus welchen zärtlich entblätterten Blüten-Kelchen
reifen die fremdartigen Früchte der Tröstung? Diese
köstlichen, deren du eine vielleicht in der zertretenen Wiese

deiner Armut findest. Von einem zum anderen Male
wunderst du dich über die Größe der Frucht,
über ihr Heilsein, über die Sanftheit der Schale,
und daß sie der Leichtsinn des Vogels dir nicht vorweg-
nahm und nicht die Eifersucht

unten des Wurms. Giebt es denn Bäume, von Engeln beflogen,
und von verborgenen langsamen Gärtnern so seltsam gezogen,
daß sie uns tragen, ohne uns zu gehören?

Haben wir niemals vermocht, wir Schatten und Schemen,
durch unser voreilig reifes und wieder welkes Benehmen
jener gelassenen Sommer Gleichmut zu stören?

II.17

Where, in what blissfully-watered gardens,
on which trees, from what soft opening blossoms
do the wild fruits of solace ripen? Precious
fruit, which may be found in the trampled meadows

of your losses. Time and again, you find
yourself astonished by the size of the fruit,
by its wholeness and its unbroken rind –
when no lax bird or jealous worm at the root

has taken it. Are there trees where angels gather,
cultivated by slow, unknowable gardeners,
that give us fruit although they are not ours?

We soon grow ripe, then wither, just like phantoms
or shadows. Don't we ever possess the power
to ruffle the stillness of these tranquil summers?

II.18

Tänzerin: o du Verlegung
alles Vergehens in Gang: wie brachtest du's dar.
Und der Wirbel am Schluß, dieser Baum aus Bewegung,
nahm er nicht ganz in Besitz das erschwungene Jahr?

Blühte nicht, daß ihn dein Schwingen von vorhin umschwärme,
plötzlich sein Wipfel von Stille? Und über ihr,
war sie nicht Sonne, war sie nicht Sommer, die Wärme,
diese unzählige Wärme aus dir?

Aber er trug auch, er trug, dein Baum der Ekstase.
Sind sie nicht seine ruhigen Früchte: der Krug,
reifend gestreift, und die gereiftere Vase?

Und in den Bildern: ist nicht die Zeichnung geblieben,
die deiner Braue dunkler Zug
rasch an die Wandung der eigenen Wendung geschrieben?

II.18

Dancer: oh, you translation
of all things fleeting into steps.
And how! That last whirl, tree of motion –
wasn't the sweep of the year possessed?

Didn't the wavering swarm at its top,
all in blossom, at once become calm?
Overhead, wasn't it summer and sun,
from your measureless radiant warmth?

It also bore your tree of ecstasy.
Aren't these its peaceful fruits: the urn,
with its ripening bars, and the seasoned vase?

And in these pictures: doesn't the sketch endure,
the dark line of your eyebrows penciling
quickly – across the turning page?

II.19

Irgendwo wohnt das Gold in der verwöhnenden Bank,
und mit Tausenden tut es vertraulich. Doch jener
Blinde, der Bettler, ist selbst dem kupfernen Zehner
wie ein verlorener Ort, wie das staubige Eck unterm Schrank.

In den Geschäften entlang ist das Geld wie zuhause
und verkleidet sich scheinbar in Seide, Nelken und Pelz.
Er, der Schweigende, steht in der Atempause
alles des wach oder schlafend atmenden Gelds.

O wie mag sie sich schließen bei Nacht, diese immer offene Hand.
Morgen holt sie das Schicksal wieder, und täglich
hält es sie hin: hell, elend, unendlich zerstörbar.

Daß doch einer, ein Schauender, endlich ihren langen Bestand
staunend begriffe und rühmte. Nur dem Aufsingenden säglich.
Nur dem Göttlichen hörbar.

II.19

Gold resides in some indulgent bank,
intimate with many. But for the blind
beggar, a copper coin is like a place
that's lost, a dusty corner he can't find.

Money feels right at home in all the stores;
it struts by, dressed in silk, fur, and carnations.
He, the silent one, dwells within the lulls
that breathing money makes, asleep or awakened.

How can it close, that ever-open hand?
When the night ends, fate brings it out once more:
wretched, easily destructible.

Until some shocked onlooker understands,
and praises its duration. A singer can say.
Only for a god is it audible.

II.20

Zwischen den Sternen, wie weit; und doch, um wievieles noch weiter,
was man am Hiesigen lernt.
Einer, zum Beispiel, ein Kind ... und ein Nächster, ein Zweiter –,
o wie unfaßlich entfernt.

Schicksal, es mißt uns vielleicht mit des Seienden Spanne,
daß es uns fremd erscheint;
denk, wieviel Spannen allein vom Mädchen zum Manne,
wenn es ihn meidet und meint.

Alles ist weit –, und nirgends schließt sich der Kreis.
Sieh in der Schüssel, auf heiter bereitetem Tische,
seltsam der Fische Gesicht.

Fische sind stumm ..., meinte man einmal. Wer weiß?
Aber ist nicht am Ende ein Ort, wo man das, was der Fische
Sprache wäre, *ohne* sie spricht?

II.20

How far between the stars; and yet, much farther
are the distances that we grasp this instant.
Just look at any child . . . and then, another
– oh, how inexpressibly distant.

Maybe fate measures us in spans of being,
and for this reason it seems inauspicious;
How many spans might separate the woman
who flees from that same man she also wishes.

All is far; the circle's incomplete.
Look at that fish waiting for us to eat:
how strange is its expression in the dish!

Fish are mute . . . or so we thought. Who knows?
Isn't there a place where the language of the fish,
or what it would be, can at last be spoken?

II.21

Singe die Gärten, mein Herz, die du nicht kennst; wie in Glas
eingegossene Gärten, klar, unerreichbar.
Wasser und Rosen von Ispahan oder Schiras,
singe sie selig, preise sie, keinem vergleichbar.

Zeige, mein Herz, daß du sie niemals entbehrst.
Daß sie dich meinen, ihre reifenden Feigen.
Daß du mit ihren, zwischen den blühenden Zweigen
wie zum Gesicht gesteigerten Lüften verkehrst.

Meide den Irrtum, daß es Entbehrungen gebe
für den geschehnen Entschluß, diesen: zu sein!
Seidener Faden, kamst du hinein ins Gewebe.

Welchem der Bilder du auch im Innern geeint bist
(sei es selbst ein Moment aus dem Leben der Pein),
fühl, daß der ganze, der rühmliche Teppich gemeint ist.

II.21

Sing, my heart, of gardens you've never known;
clear, inaccessible, as if encased
in glass. Waters and roses of Shiraz
or Isfahan: rejoice, for they are graced

supremely. Show that you cannot do without them,
and that their figs are ripening for you.
You are familiar with the winds among
the pregnant branches looming into view.

Avoid the mistake of thinking you offended
fate through this decision: to exist!
Silk thread, into the fabric you were blended.

Whatever shape you inwardly go into
(even one moment from a life of pain),
know that the whole tapestry is intended.

II.22

O trotz Schicksal: die herrlichen Überflüsse
unseres Daseins, in Parken übergeschäumt, –
oder als steinerne Männer neben die Schlüsse
hoher Portale, unter Balkone gebäumt!

O die eherne Glocke, die ihre Keule
täglich wider den stumpfen Alltag hebt.
Oder die *eine*, in Karnak, die Säule, die Säule,
die fast ewige Tempel überlebt.

Heute stürzen die Überschüsse, dieselben,
nur noch als Eile vorbei, aus dem waagrechten gelben
Tag in die blendend mit Licht übertriebene Nacht.

Aber das Rasen zergeht und läßt keine Spuren.
Kurven des Flugs durch die Luft und die, die sie fuhren,
keine vielleicht ist umsonst. Doch nur wie gedacht.

II.22

Oh despite fate: the lavish extravagance
of our existence, gushing like fountains in parks
– or taking form as stone men propping up
tall entrances, and under lofty walks!

And the bronze bell, lifting up its hammer
against the dull routine of everydayness. . . .
Or at Karnak that column there – the one
that has outlasted temples that are ancient.

Today those same abundances will race
away, the fast ones, going straight across
from yellow day to overwhelming night.

The frenzy passes by without a trace.
But they survive, those lovely arcs of flight
and those who made them – only in our thoughts.

II.23

Rufe mich zu jener deiner Stunden,
die dir unaufhörlich widersteht:
flehend nah wie das Gesicht von Hunden,
aber immer wieder weggedreht,

wenn du meinst, sie endlich zu erfassen.
So Entzognes ist am meisten dein.
Wir sind frei. Wir wurden dort entlassen,
wo wir meinten, erst begrüßt zu sein.

Bang verlangen wir nach einem Halte,
wir zu Jungen manchmal für das Alte
und zu alt für das, was niemals war.

Wir, gerecht nur, wo wir dennoch preisen,
weil wir, ach, der Ast sind und das Eisen
und das Süße reifender Gefahr.

II.23

Summon me to the one among your hours
which resists you, time and time again:
as a dog's face gently begs, then cowers,
turning away (it always does) just when

you think at last that it's within your reach.
What's taken away like this is most your own;
we're free, because we found ourselves released
just where we thought of being welcomed home.

Anxiously we grapple for a hold –
sometimes, we're too young for what is old
and too old for that which never was.

Still, it's only fair to praise, because:
oh, nonetheless. We are the metal, and
the sweet that looms and ripens on the branch.

II.24

O diese Lust, immer neu, aus gelockertem Lehm!
Niemand beinah hat den frühesten Wagern geholfen.
Städte entstanden trotzdem an beseligten Golfen,
Wasser und Öl füllten die Krüge trotzdem.

Götter, wir planen sie erst in erkühnten Entwürfen,
die uns das mürrische Schicksal wieder zerstört.
Aber sie sind die Unsterblichen. Sehet, wir dürfen
jenen erhorchen, der uns am Ende erhört.

Wir, ein Geschlecht durch Jahrtausende: Mütter und Väter,
immer erfüllter von dem künftigen Kind,
daß es uns einst, übersteigend, erschüttere, später.

Wir, wir unendlich Gewagten, was haben wir Zeit!
Und nur der schweigsame Tod, der weiß, was wir sind
und was er immer gewinnt, wenn er uns leiht.

II.24

Oh this ever-new urge, from loosened soil!
At first, no one would help those daring few;
but still, on lucky gulfs, the cities grew
and jugs filled nonetheless with water and oil.

Gods: we draw them first in the boldest colors,
which sullen fate eventually destroys.
And yet they *are* immortal. Our reward
is to hear that one who attends to us.

We are one generation through the ages,
fathers and mothers filled with kids to come
so that, at last, we shall be overtaken.

We, always daring – Time is never done!
And only silent Death can keep in mind
the victory he wins by lending time.

II.25

Schon, horch, hörst du der ersten Harken
Arbeit; wieder den menschlichen Takt
in der verhaltenen Stille der starken
Vorfrühlingserde. Unabgeschmackt

scheint dir das Kommende. Jenes so oft
dir schon Gekommene scheint dir zu kommen
wieder wie Neues. Immer erhofft,
nahmst du es niemals. Es hat dich genommen.

Selbst die Blätter durchwinterter Eichen
scheinen im Abend ein künftiges Braun.
Manchmal geben sich Lüfte ein Zeichen.

Schwarz sind die Sträucher. Doch Haufen von Dünger
lagern als satteres Schwarz in den Aun.
Jede Stunde, die hingeht, wird jünger.

II.25

Listen – already you can hear at work
the first plows turning, and the gentle strum
of human measures on the pregnant earth
before a robust spring. What's bound to come

does not seem free of taste. What often showed
itself before appears to arrive anew,
as something else. Forever well-disposed,
you never took it in – but it took you.

Even the leaves of wintering trees reveal
a glimpse at dusk presaging later brown.
Sometimes, even the winds make their appeal.

Black are the bushes. Still, the heaps of dung
stand blacker all across the fertile ground.
And each elapsing hour grows more young.

II.26

Wie ergreift uns der Vogelschrei . . .
Irgendein einmal erschaffenes Schreien.
Aber die Kinder schon, spielend im Freien,
schreien an wirklichen Schreien vorbei.

Schreien den Zufall. In Zwischenräume
dieses, des Weltraums, (in welchen der heile
Vogelschrei eingeht, wie Menschen in Träume –)
treiben sie ihre, des Kreischens, Keile.

Wehe, wo sind wir? Immer noch freier,
wie die losgerissenen Drachen
jagen wir halbhoch, mit Rändern von Lachen,

windig zerfetzten. – Ordne die Schreier,
singender Gott! daß sie rauschend erwachen,
tragend als Strömung das Haupt und die Leier.

II.26

How we are moved by the call of a bird . . .
or any other cry, once it's been made.
Even the brightest kids, who play
out in the open, surpass what's actually heard.

Contingent scream. In all these gaps between,
this world-space (where bird-cries enter
unashamed, as men go into dreams) –
their shrieks are driven in, like wedges.

Alas, where are we? Always more free,
and laughter-edged, like kites with broken string,
we range halfway across the sky

wind-ripped. Oh Poet, orchestrate all those
who cry: may they awaken with a roar,
one current carrying both head and lyre.

II.27

Giebt es wirklich die Zeit, die zerstörende?
Wann, auf dem ruhenden Berg, zerbricht sie die Burg?
Dieses Herz, das unendlich den Göttern gehörende,
wann vergewaltigts der Demiurg?

Sind wir wirklich so ängstlich Zerbrechliche,
wie das Schicksal uns wahr machen will?
Ist die Kindheit, die tiefe, versprechliche,
in den Wurzeln – später – still?

Ach, das Gespenst des Vergänglichen,
durch den arglos Empfänglichen
geht es, als wär es ein Rauch.

Als die, die wir sind, als die Treibenden,
gelten wir doch bei bleibenden
Kräften als göttlicher Brauch.

II.27

Is there such a thing as Time the destroyer?
When will it wreck the tower on the mountain?
As for this heart, so far divinely owned,
when does it fall to the Demiurge's power?

Are we really so anxiously breakable
as our Destiny seems to indicate?
Must childhood, so deep and capable,
eventually get cut off at the base?

Ah, the ghost of transience –
it goes right through the innocent
as if it were passing through haze.

And as for us, the ones who strive,
the powers assign us a role to play
as part of the godly enterprise.

II.28

O komm und geh. Du, fast noch Kind, ergänze
für einen Augenblick die Tanzfigur
zum reinen Sternbild einer jener Tänze,
darin wir die dumpf ordnende Natur

vergänglich übertreffen. Denn sie regte
sich völlig hörend nur, da Orpheus sang.
Du warst noch die von damals her Bewegte
und leicht befremdet, wenn ein Baum sich lang

besann, mit dir nach dem Gehör zu gehn.
Du wußtest noch die Stelle, wo die Leier
sich tönend hob –; die unerhörte Mitte.

Für sie versuchtest du die schönen Schritte
und hofftest, einmal zu der heilen Feier
des Freundes Gang und Antlitz hinzudrehn.

II.28

Oh, come and go. You, almost still a child,
perform a dance in the blink of an eye, creating
a pure constellation – one of those
devices by which orderly, blunt Nature

is momently surpassed. For she was stirred
to total hearing only by Orphic song.
You were inspired from the time you heard,
and thought it odd if any tree stood long

before it joined you in the space of hearing.
You still remember where the lyre arose,
intoning – from that middlemost location.

Therefore, you took exquisite steps, and hoped
eventually to bring your friend to peer
and step into the sacred celebration.

II.29

Stiller Freund der vielen Fernen, fühle,
wie dein Atem noch den Raum vermehrt.
Im Gebälk der finstern Glockenstühle
lass dich läuten. Das, was an dir zehrt,

wird ein Starkes über dieser Nahrung.
Geh in der Verwandlung aus und ein.
Was ist deine leidendste Erfahrung?
Ist dir Trinken bitter, werde Wein.

Sei in dieser Nacht aus Übermaß
Zauberkraft am Kreuzweg deiner Sinne,
ihrer seltsamen Begegnung Sinn.

Und wenn dich das Irdische vergaß,
zu der stillen Erde sag: Ich rinne.
Zu dem raschen Wasser sprich: Ich bin.

II.29

Quiet friend of many distances,
feel how your breath is creating room.
Among the rafters of dark belfries let
yourself ring out. Whatever's eating you

is growing strong upon this offering.
Give way to transformation every time.
What experience brings your deepest suffering?
If your drinking is bitter, turn to wine.

In this comprehensive night, become
the junction where all senses intermix;
be the truth of their odd rendezvous.

And if the world has forgotten you,
say this to the stable earth: I run.
Tell the rushing water: I exist.

Coda: from the Late French Poems

Dire une Fleure

La terre comment fait-elle pour, en sa profondeur
terrible et tragique dont on a peur,
préparer la candeur d'une fleur heureuse?
Hélas, mon cœur est creux, ma main est creuse,
que naîtra-t-il jamais de mon malheur?

Oh terre terrienne, terre pleine de morts,
apprends-moi un peu de ton audace.
Et que je fasse
printemps pareil par un pareil effort
(car il faut vivre si on vit encore).

Ne suis-je de toi? Que ta vigueur
ne me méprise point, qui tout pénètre,
ma tête est triste mais j'ai le cœur champêtre;
il se pourrait bien que je dise une fleur.

To Speak a Flower

Within its terrible and tragic depth –
which frightens us – how is it that the earth
prepares the frankness of a happy flower?
Alas, my hand is empty, so is my heart;
whatever will be born of my distress?

Oh earthly soil, earth replete with death,
teach me how I can apprehend a little
of your audacity. And may I make
spring the same way, with your same power
(for if we're still alive, then we must live).

Do I not come from you? May your strength
not scorn me, as it permeates all things;
my head is sad, but I have a pastoral
heart. I very well might speak a flower.